Herr Battler

GENEVA

a fancied page of history in three acts by

Bernard Shaw

illustrated by Feliks Topolski

CONSTABLE & CO LTD LONDON

PUBLISHED BY
Constable and Company Ltd.
LONDON

The Macmillan Company
of Canada, Limited
TORONTO

First published June 1939
Reprinted   June 1939
New Edition February 1940

PRINTED IN GREAT BRITAIN AT THE CHISWICK PRESS LTD.
NEW SOUTHGATE LONDON N.11

LIST OF ILLUSTRATIONS

This play was first presented by Roy Limbert at the Malvern Festival on August 1st, 1938, with the following cast:

BEGONIA BROWN	Eileen Beldon
THE JEW	Donald Eccles
A NEWCOMER	Maitland Moss
THE WIDOW	Phyllis Gill
A JOURNALIST	Wilson Barrett
THE BISHOP	H. R. Hignett
COMMISSAR POSKY	J. O. Twiss
THE SECRETARY OF THE LEAGUE OF NATIONS	Cyril Gardiner
SIR ORPHEUS MIDLANDER	Ernest Thesiger
THE BETROTHED	Kenneth Villiers
THE JUDGE	Donald Wolfit
BOMBARDONE	Cecil Trouncer
BATTLER	Norman Wooland
THE DEACONESS	Marie Ault
GENERAL FLANCO DE FORTINBRAS	R. Stuart Lindsell

The play produced by H. K. Ayliff

The play was produced at the Saville Theatre, London, on November 22nd, 1938, with the following cast:

BEGONIA BROWN	Alison Leggatt
A JEW	Donald Eccles
A NEWCOMER	William Heilbronn
A WIDOW	Phillippa Gill
A JOURNALIST	Tom Anstead
A BISHOP	H. R. Hignett
COMMISSAR POSKY	Arthur Ridley
THE SECRETARY OF THE LEAGUE OF NATIONS	Cyril Gardiner
SIR ORPHEUS MIDLANDER	Ernest Thesiger
THE JUDGE	Alexander Knox
THE BETROTHED	Tully Comber
BOMBARDONE	Cecil Trouncer
BATTLER	Walter Hudd
A DEACONESS	Olive Milbourne
GENERAL FLANCO DE FORTINBRAS	R. Stuart Lindsell

GENEVA

ACT I

*A May morning in Geneva, in a meagrely equipped
office with secondhand furniture, much the worse for wear,
consisting of a dingy writing table with an old typewriter
on it in the middle of the room, a revolving chair for the
typist, an old press which has not been painted or var-
nished for many years, and three chairs for visitors against
the wall near the door. The stove, an undecorated iron one*

of the plainest sort, designed rather for central heating in a cellar than for an inhabited apartment, is to the typist's right, the press facing it at the opposite side on the typist's left. The door is beside the press. The window is behind the typist.

A young Englishwoman is seated in the revolving chair. From the state of the table she seems to have been working at the compilation of a card index, as there are cards scattered about, and an open case to put them in, also a pile of foolscap from which she has been copying the card inscriptions. But at present she is not at work. She is smoking and reading an illustrated magazine with her heels on the table. A thermos flask, a cup and saucer, and a packet of cigarettes are beside her on a sliding shelf drawn out from the table. She is a self-satisfied young person, fairly attractive and well aware of it. Her dress, though smartly cut, is factory made; and her speech and manners are London suburban.

Somebody knocks at the door. She hastily takes her heels off the table; jumps up; throws her cigarette into the stove; snatches the things off the sliding shelf and hides them in the press; finally resumes her seat and looks as busy as possible.

THE TYPIST [*calling*] Entrez, s'il vous plaît.

A middle-aged gentleman of distinguished appearance, with a blond beard and moustache, top hatted, frock coated, and gloved, comes in. He contemplates the room and the young woman with evident surprise.

HE. Pardon, mademoiselle: I seek the office of the International Committee for Intellectual Co-operation.

SHE. Yes: thats quite all right. Take a seat, please.

HE [*hesitating*] Thank you; but my business is of great importance: I must see your chief. This is not the head office, is it?

SHE. No: the head office is in Paris. This is all there is here. Not much of a place, is it?

HE. Well, I must confess that after visiting the magnificent palace of the International Labor Office and the new quarters of the Secretariat, I expected to find the Committee for Intellectual Co-operation lodged in some imposingly monumental structure.

SHE. Oh, isnt it scandalous? I wish youd write to the papers about it. Do please sit down.

HE. Thank you. [*He is about to take one of the chairs from the wall*].

SHE. No, not that one: one of its legs isnt safe: it's there only for show. Will you please take the other?

HE. Can the Committee not afford you a new chair?

SHE. It cant afford anything. The intellectual budget is the interest on two million paper francs that one is glad to get threepence for: they used to be tuppence. So here I am in one rotten little room on the third floor of a tumbledown old house full of rats. And as to my salary I should be ashamed to name it. A Church charity would be ashamed to pay it.

HE. I am utterly astounded. [*He takes a sound chair from the wall; places it near the office table; and sits down*]. The intellectual co-operation of sixty nations must be a very extensive business. How can it possibly be conducted in this bare little place?

SHE. Oh, I conduct it all right. It's never in a hurry, you know.

3

HE. But really—pardon me if I am taking too much of your time—

SHE. Oh, thats quite all right. I'm only too glad to have a bit of chat with somebody. Nobody ever comes in here: people dont seem to know that the Committee exists.

HE. Do you mean that you have nothing to do?

SHE. Oh no. I tell you I have to do all the intellectual co-operation. I have to do it singlehanded too: I havnt even an office boy to help me. And theres no end to the work. If it werent, as I say, that theres no hurry about it, I should never get through it. Just look here at this nice little job theyve given me! A card index of all the universities with the names and addresses of their bursars and their vice chancellors. And there is a correspondence about the protection of professional titles that takes up half my time.

HE. And do they call that intellectual co-operation?

SHE. Well, what else would you call it?

HE. It is mere compilation. How are the intellectual giants who form your committee bringing the enormous dynamic force of their brains, their prestige, their authority, to bear on the destinies of the nations? What are they doing to correct the mistakes of our ignorant politicians?

SHE. Well, we have their names on our notepaper, you know. What more can they do? You cant expect them to sit in this little hole talking to people. I have never seen one of them.

HE. So they leave it all to you?

SHE. Oh, I wouldnt say all. Theres the head office in Paris, you know, and some offices in other coun-

4

Begonia Brown

tries. I suppose they do their bit; and anyhow we all do a lot of writing to oneanother. But I must say it's as dull as ditchwater. When I took the job I thought it was going to be interesting, and that I'd see all the great men. I am ambitious, you know: I won a London County Council scholarship. I wanted a job that would draw out my faculties, if you understand me. But theres nothing to do here that any common typist couldnt do. And nobody ever comes near the place. Oh, it is dull.

HE. Shall I give you an interesting job, mademoiselle? One that would get you appreciated and perhaps a little talked about?

SHE. I'll just jump at it—if it is all right.

HE. How all right?

SHE. Morally, you know. No hanky panky. I am respectable; and I mean to keep respectable.

HE. I pledge you my word that my intentions are completely honorable.

SHE. Well, what about the pay? And how long will the job last? The work here may be dull; and the pay is just short of starvation; but I have the appointment for 25 years certain; and I darent give it up for anything chancy. You dont know what it is to be out of a job.

HE. I shall not ask you to give up your post here. On the contrary, it is essential that you should keep it. But I think I can make it more interesting for you. And I should of course make you a suitable present if at any time you found that your emoluments here were insufficient.

SHE. They are. But I mustnt take bribes, you know.

HE. You need not.
Any friendly service
I may be able to ren-
der will be entirely
independent of your
official work here.

SHE. Look here: I
dont half like this.
Whats the game?

THE JEW. I must
begin by explaining
that I am a Jew.

SHE. I dont believe
you. You dont look
like one.

THE JEW. I am not
a primitive Hittite.
You cannot draw my nose in profile by simply
writing down the number six. My hair is not black,
nor do I wear it in excessively oiled ringlets. I have
all the marks of a German blond. German is my
native language: in fact I am in every sense a German. But I worship in the synagogue; and when I
worship I put my hat on, whereas a German takes
it off. On this ground they class me as a non-Aryan,
which is nonsense, as there is no such thing as an
Aryan.

SHE. I'm so glad to hear you say that. The Germans
here say that I am an Aryan; but I tell them I am nothing of the kind: I'm an Englishwoman. Not a common Englishwoman, of course: I'm a Camberwell
woman; and though the west end may turn up its nose

at Camberwell, Camberwell is better than Peckham any day in the week.

THE JEW. No doubt. I have not been there.

SHE. I never could abide Peckham people. They are disliked everywhere. It's instinctive, somehow. Havnt you noticed it?

THE JEW. All peoples are disliked in the lump. The English are disliked: the Germans are disliked: the French are disliked. The Protestants are disliked; and all their hundreds of sects dislike one another. So are the Catholics, the Jesuits, the Freemasons. You tell me that the inhabitants of Peckham are disliked: no doubt they deserve it.

SHE. They do.

THE JEW. Some of the greatest men have disliked the human race. But for Noah, its Creator would have drowned it. Can we deny that He had good reasons for disliking it? Can I deny that there are good reasons for disliking Jews? On the contrary, I dislike most of them myself.

SHE. Oh dont say that. Ive known lots of quite nice Jews. What I say is why pick on the Jews, as if they were any worse than other people?

THE JEW. That is precisely my business here today. I find you most intelligent—most sympathetic.

SHE. Come now! none of that. Whats the game?

THE JEW. I have been assaulted, plundered, and driven from my native soil by its responsible ruler. I, as a ruined individual, can do nothing. But the League of Nations can act through its Committee for Intellectual Co-operation. The Committee can act through the permanent court of International Justice at the

7

Hague, which is also an organ of the League. My business here is to ask the Committee to apply to the court for a warrant against the responsible ruler. I charge him with assault and battery, burglary—

SHE. Burglary! Did they break into your house?

THE JEW. I cannot speak of it. Everything I treasured. Wrecked! Smashed! Defiled! Never will I forgive: never can I forget.

SHE. But why didnt you call the police?

THE JEW. Mademoiselle: the police did it. The Government did it. The Dictator who controls the police is responsible before Europe! before civilization! I look to the League of Nations for redress. It alone can call unrighteous rulers to account. The initiative must be taken by its Committee for Intellectual Co-operation: that is, for the moment, by you, mademoiselle.

SHE. But what can I do? I cant go out and collar your unrighteous ruler.

THE JEW. No, mademoiselle. What you must do is to write to the International Court, calling on it to issue a warrant for the arrest of my oppressor on a charge of attempting to exterminate a section of the human race.

SHE. Well, it seems like taking a lot on myself, doesnt it?

THE JEW. Not at all. You will be acting, not for yourself, but for the intellect of Europe. I assure you it is the correct course.

SHE. But I'm not sure that I know how to write a letter with all those police court things in it.

THE JEW. It is quite simple. But if you will allow me I will draft the letter for you.

SHE. Oh I say, Mister Jew, I dont like this.

THE JEW. Then write the letter yourself. I am sure you will do it perfectly. It will be an opportunity for you to shew the Committee what you are made of.

SHE. Well, look here. I have a particular friend, an American journalist. Would you mind if I shewed him your draft before I send it off?

THE JEW. An American journalist! Excellent, excellent. By all means submit my draft to him and ask him to correct it if necessary. My English is German English, and may leave something to be desired.

SHE. Yes: thatll be splendid. Thank you ever so much.

THE JEW. Not at all. [*Rising*] I will bring the draft in the course of the afternoon. Au revoir, then.

SHE. Au revoir.

They shake hands cordially. Meanwhile the door is opened by an obstinate-looking middle-aged man of respectable but not aristocratic appearance, speaking English like a shopkeeper from the provinces, or perhaps, by emigration, the dominions.

NEWCOMER. Can I see the boss, miss?

9

SHE [*with haughty nonchalance in a would-be distinguished accent startlingly unlike her unaffected deference
to the gentlemanlike Jew*] I am sorry. Our chiefs are
scattered over Europe, very eminent persons, you
know. Can I do anything?

NEWCOMER [*looking at the Jewish gentleman*] I'm
afraid I'm interrupting.

THE JEW. Not at all: my business is finished. [*Click-
ing his heels and bowing*] Until the afternoon, mademoiselle. Monsieur—[*He bows to the newcomer, and
goes out*].

SHE. You can sit down.

NEWCOMER. I will keep you only a minute, miss.
[*He sits and takes out some notes he has made*].

SHE. Be as quick as you can, please. I am busy this
morning.

NEWCOMER. Yes: you have the brainwork of the
world on your shoulders here. When any of the
nations goes off the rails, this is the place to have it put
back. Thats so, isnt it?

SHE [*with aplomb*] Undoubtedly.

NEWCOMER. Well, it's like this. In my country
weve had an election. We thought it lay between our
usual people: the National Party and the Labor Party;
but it was won by an upstart kind of chap who called
himself a Business Democrat. He got a clear majority
over the Nationals and the Labor Party; so it was up
to him to form a Government. And what do you suppose the fellow did when he became Prime Minister?

SHE [*bored*] Cant imagine, I'm sure.

NEWCOMER. He said he had been returned to power
as a business democrat, and that the business part of it

meant that he was not to waste time, but to get the nation's work done as quickly as possible.

SHE. Quite, quite. Nothing to complain of in that, is there?

NEWCOMER. Wait. I'm going to astonish you. He said the country had decided by its democratic vote that it should be governed by him and his party for the next five years, and that no opposition could be tolerated. He said the defeated minority must step down and out instead of staying there to obstruct and delay and annoy him. Of course the Opposition werent going to stand that: they refused to leave the Chamber. So he adjourned the House until next day; and when the Opposition turned up the police wouldnt let them in. Most of them couldnt get as far as the doors, because the Prime Minister had organized a body of young men called the Clean Shirts, to help the police.

SHE. Well?

NEWCOMER. Well!!! Is that all you have to say to me?

SHE. What do you expect me to say? It seems all right to me. It's what any man of business would do. Wouldnt you?

NEWCOMER. Of course I should do it in business; but this is politics.

SHE. Well! arnt politics business?

NEWCOMER. Of course theyre not. Just the opposite. You know that, dont you?

SHE. Oh, quite, quite.

NEWCOMER. What I say is, business methods are business methods; and parliamentary methods are parliamentary methods.

SHE [*brightly*] "And never the twain shall meet", as Kipling puts it.

NEWCOMER. No: I dont hold with Kipling. Too imperialist for me. I'm a democrat.

SHE. But not a business democrat, if I follow you.

NEWCOMER. No, no: not a business democrat. A proper democrat. I'm all for the rights of minorities.

SHE. But I always thought that democracy meant the right of the majority to have its way.

NEWCOMER. Oh no: that would be the end of all liberty. You have nothing to say against liberty, I hope.

SHE. I have nothing to say against anything. I am not here to discuss politics with everyone who walks into my office. What do you want?

NEWCOMER. Well, heres a Prime Minister committing high treason and rebellion and breach of privilege; levying armed forces against the Crown; violating the constitution; setting up a dictatorship and obstructing the lawful ingress of duly elected members to the legislative Chamber. Whats to be done with him?

SHE. Quite simple. I shall apply to the International Court at the Hague for a warrant for his arrest on all those charges. You can look in at the end of the week, when the answer from the Hague will have arrived. You will supply me with the man's name and the particulars—

NEWCOMER [*putting his notes on the table before her*]

The Zero

Here they are, miss. By Gosh, thats a splendid idea.

SHE. Thank you. That is all. Good morning.

NEWCOMER [*rising and going to the door*] Well, you know how to do business here: theres no mistake about that. Good morning, miss.

As he is going out the door opens in his face; and a widow comes in: a Creole lady of about forty, with the remains of a gorgeous and opulent southern beauty. Her imposing style and dress at once reduce the young lady of the office to nervous abjection.

THE WIDOW. Are you the president of the Intellectual Co-operation Committee of the League of Nations?

NEWCOMER. No, maam. This lady will do all you require [*he goes out*].

THE WIDOW. Am I to take that seriously? My business is important. I came here to place it before a body of persons of European distinction. I am not prepared to discuss it with an irresponsible young woman.

SHE. I am afraid I dont look the part, do I? I am only the staff, so to speak. Still, anything I can do I shall be most happy.

THE WIDOW. But where are your chiefs?

SHE. Ah, there you have me. They live all over the world, as you might say.

THE WIDOW. But do they not come here to attend to their business?

SHE. Well, you see, there is really nothing for them to attend to. It's only intellectual business, you know.

THE WIDOW. But do they not take part in the Assembly of the League?

B   13

SHE. Some of them have been, once. Nobody ever goes to the Assembly twice if they can help it.

THE WIDOW. But I must see somebody—somebody of importance.

SHE. Well, I'm sorry. Theres nobody but me. I can do whatever is necessary. Did you by any chance want a warrant from the International Court at the Hague?

THE WIDOW. Yes: that is exactly what I do want. A death warrant.

SHE. A what?!!

THE WIDOW. A death warrant. I will sit down, if you will allow me.

SHE. Oh please—

THE WIDOW [*sitting down*] Do you see that? [*She takes an automatic pistol from her bag, and throws it on the table*].

SHE. Oh, thats not allowed in Geneva. Put it up quick. Somebody might come in.

THE WIDOW [*replacing the pistol in her bag*] This is the most absurd place. In my country everybody carries a gun.

SHE. What country, may I ask?

THE WIDOW. The Republic of the Earthly Paradise.

SHE. My mother has a school prize called The Earthly Paradise. What a coincidence!

THE WIDOW. Then you know that the Earthly Paradise is one of the leading States in the world in culture

14

and purity of race, and that its capital contained more than two thousand white inhabitants before the last revolution. There must be still at least fifteen hundred left.

SHE. But is it a member of the League?

THE WIDOW. Of course it is. And allow me to remind you that by its veto it can put a stop to all action by the League until its affairs are properly attended to.

SHE. Can it? I didnt know that. Of course I shall be only too pleased to apply for a warrant; but I'd rather not call it a death warrant. Death warrant sounds a bit thick, if you understand me. All you need do is to give me a list of the charges you make against—well, against whoever it is.

THE WIDOW. Simply one charge of the wilful murder of my late husband by the President of the Earthly Paradise.

SHE. Surely if a president kills anyone it's an execution; but if anyone kills a president it's an assassination.

THE WIDOW. And is not that just the state of things the League of Nations is here to put a stop to?

SHE. Oh, dont ask me. All I know about the League is that it pays my salary. Just give me the gentleman's name and who he murdered. Murder stories are thrillingly interesting.

THE WIDOW. You would not think so if you lived in a country where there is at least one murder in every family.

SHE. What an awful place! Is it as barbarous as that?

THE WIDOW. Barbarous! Certainly not. The

Earthly Paradise is the most civilized country in the world. Its constitution is absolutely democratic: every president must swear to observe it in every particular. The Church is abolished: no moral authority is recognized except that of the people's will. The president and parliament are elected by adult suffrage every two years. So are all the judges and all the officials, even the road sweepers. All these reforms, which have made The Earthly Paradise the most advanced member of the League of Nations, were introduced by my late husband the sixth president. He observed the constitution strictly. The elections were conducted with absolute integrity. The ballot was secret. The people felt free for the first time in their lives. Immediately after the elections the budget was passed providing for two years. My husband then prorogued the Parliament until the end of that period, and governed the country according to his own ideas whilst the people enjoyed themselves and made money in their own ways without any political disturbances or arguments. He was re-elected three times, and is now known in the Paradise as the father of his country.

SHE. But you said he was murdered, and that the president murdered him. How could that be if he was the president? He couldnt murder himself.

THE WIDOW. Unhappily he had certain weaknesses. He was an affectionate husband: I may even say an uxorious one; but he was very far from being faithful to me. When he abolished the Church he would have abolished marriage also if public opinion would have stood for it. And he was much too indulgent to his enemies. Naturally, whenever he won an election his opponent raised an army and attempted a revolution; for we are a high spirited race and do not submit to the insult of defeat at the polls. But my husband was a military genius. He had no difficulty in putting down these revolutions; but instead of having his opponent shot in the proper and customary way, he pardoned him and challenged him to try again as often as he pleased. I urged him again and again not to trifle with his own safety in this way. Useless: he would not listen to me. At last I found out the reason. He was carrying on an intrigue with his opponent's wife, my best friend. I had to shoot her—shoot her dead—my dearest friend [*she is overcome with emotion*].

SHE. Oh, you shouldnt have done that. That was going a little too far, wasnt it?

THE WIDOW. Public opinion obliged me to do it as a self-respecting wife and mother. God knows I did not want to do it: I loved her: I would have let her have ten husbands if I had had them to give. But what can you do against the etiquette of your class? My brothers had to fight duels and kill their best friends because it was etiquette.

SHE. But where were the police? Werent you tried for it?

THE WIDOW. Of course I was tried for it; but I pleaded the unwritten law and was acquitted. Unfortunately the scandal destroyed my husband's popularity. He was defeated at the next election by the man he had so foolishly spared. Instead of raising an army to avenge this outrage, my husband, crushed by the loss of his mistress, just moped at home until they came and shot him. They had come to shoot me; and [*with a fresh burst of tears*] I wish to Heaven they had; but I was out at the time; so they thought they might as well shoot my husband as there was nobody else to shoot.

SHE. What a dreadful thing for you!

THE WIDOW. Not at all. It served him right, absolutely. He never spoke to me after I had to kill the woman we both loved more than we loved oneanother. I believe he would have been only too glad if they had shot me; and I dont blame him. What is the use of the League of Nations if it cannot put a stop to such horrors?

SHE. Well, it's not the League's business, is it?

THE WIDOW. Not the League's business! Do you realize, young woman, that if the League does not bring the murderer of my husband to justice my son will be obliged to take up a blood feud and shoot the murderer with his own hands, though they were at the same school and are devoted to oneanother? It is against Nature, against God: if your committee does not stop it I will shoot every member of it, and you too. [*She rises*]. Excuse me. I can bear no more of this: I shall faint unless I get into the fresh air. [*She takes papers and a card from her bag and throws them on the table*]. There are the particulars. This is my card. Good morning. [*She goes as abruptly as she came in*].

SHE [*rising*] Good—

But the widow has gone and the young office lady, greatly upset, drops back into her seat with a prolonged Well!!!!!

A smart young American gentleman looks in.

THE GENTLEMAN. Say, baby: who is the old girl in

the mantilla? Carmen's grandmother, eh? [*He sits on the table edge, facing her, on the right*].

SHE. A murderess. Her dearest friend. She had to. Horrible. Theyve shot her husband. She says she will shoot me unless the League stops it.

HE. Grand! Fine!

SHE. Is that all you care? Well, look at my morning's work! Persecutions, revolutions, murders, all sorts. The office has been full of people all the morning. We shant have it all to ourselves any more.

HE. No, baby; but I shall have some dough to spend. I have been kicking my heels here for months faking news for my people when there was no news. And here you hand me a mouthful. What a scoop for me, honey! You are a peach. [*He kisses her*].

Someone knocks at the door.

SHE. Shsh! Someone knocking.

They separate hastily, he going to the stove and she composing herself in her chair.

HE. Come in! Entrez! Herein!

A gaitered English bishop enters. He is old, soft, gentle and rather infirm.

THE BISHOP. Excuse me; but does anyone here speak English?

HE [*putting on all the style he is capable of*] My native language, my lord. Also this lady's. [*Exchange of bows*]. Will you take a pew, my lord?

BISHOP [*sitting*] Thank you. Your stairs are somewhat trying to me: I am not so young as I was; and they tell me I must be careful not to overstrain my heart. The journey to Geneva is a terrible one for a man of my years. Nothing but the gravest emergency could have forced me to undertake it.

HE. Is the emergency one in which we can have the honor of assisting you, my lord?

BISHOP. Your advice would be invaluable to me; for I really dont know what to do or where to go here. I am met with indifference—with apathy—when I reveal a state of things that threatens the very existence of civilized society, of religion, of the family, of the purity of womanhood, and even, they tell me, of our commercial prosperity. Are people mad? Dont they know? Dont they care?

HE. My! my! my! [*He takes a chair to the end of the table nearest the stove*] Pray be seated, my lord. What has happened?

BISHOP [*sinking into the chair*] Sir: they are actually preaching Communism in my diocese. Communism!!! My butler, who has been in the palace for forty years, a most devoted and respectable man, tells me that my footman—I am the only bishop in England who can afford to keep a footman now—that my footman is a cell.

HE. A sell? You mean that he has disappointed you?

BISHOP. No: not that sort of cell. C.E. double L. A communist cell. Like a bee in a hive. Planted on me by the Communists to make their dreadful propaganda in my household! And my grandson at Oxford has joined a Communist club. The Union—the Oxford Union—has raised the red flag. It is dreadful. And my granddaughter a nudist! I was graciously allowed to introduce my daughters to good Queen Victoria. If she could see my granddaughter she

The Newcomer

would call the police. Is it any wonder that I have a weak heart? Shock after shock. My own footman, son of the most respectable parents, and actually an Anglo-Catholic!

HE. I can hardly believe it, my lord. What times we are living in!

SHE [*with her most official air*] Surely this is a case for the International Court at the Hague, my lord.

BISHOP. Yes, yes. An invaluable suggestion. The Court must stop the Bolshies from disseminating their horrible doctrines in England. It is in the treaties.

He is interrupted by the entrance of a very smart Russian gentleman, whom he receives with pleased recognition.

BISHOP [*rising*] Ah, my dear sir, we meet again. [*To the others*] I had the pleasure of making this gentleman's acquaintance last night at my hotel. His interest in the Church of England kept us up talking long after my usual hour for retirement. [*Shaking his hand warmly*] How do you do, my dear friend? how do you do?

RUSSIAN. Quite well, thank you, my lord. Am I interrupting your business?

BISHOP. No no no no: I beg you to remain. You will help: you will sympathize.

RUSSIAN. You are very kind, my lord: I am quite at your service.

BISHOP [*murmuring gratefully as he resumes his seat*] Thank you. Thank you.

RUSSIAN. Let me introduce myself. I am Commissar Posky of the Sovnarkom and Politbureau, Soviet delegate to the League Council.

BISHOP [*aghast, staggering to his feet*] You are a Bolshevik!

COMMISSAR. Assuredly.

The Bishop faints. General concern. The men rush to him.

COMMISSAR. Do not lift him yet. He will recover best as he is.

SHE. I have some iced lemonade in my thermos. Shall I give him some?

BISHOP [*supine*] Where am I? Has anything happened?

HE. You are in the office of the Intellectual Co-operation Committee in Geneva. You have had a slight heart attack.

COMMISSAR. Lie still, comrade. You will be quite yourself presently.

BISHOP [*sitting up*] It is not my heart. [*To the Com-*

missar] It is moral shock. You presented yourself to me yesterday as a cultivated and humane gentleman, interested in the Church of England. And now it turns out that you are a Bolshie. What right had you to practise such a cruel imposture on me? [*He rises: the Commissar helps him*] No: I can rise without assistance, thank you. [*He attempts to do so, but collapses into the arms of the Commissar*].

COMMISSAR. Steady, comrade.

BISHOP [*regaining his seat with the Commissar's assistance*] Again I must thank you. But I shudder at the touch of your bloodstained hands.

COMMISSAR. My hands are not bloodstained, comrade. I have not imposed on you. You have not quite recovered yet, I think. I am your friend of last night. Dont you recognize me?

BISHOP. A Bolshie! If I had known, sir, I should have repudiated your advances with abhorrence.

HE [*again posting himself at the stove*] Russia is a member of the League, my lord. This gentleman's standing here is the same as that of the British Foreign Secretary.

BISHOP [*intensely*] Never. Never.

SHE [*airily*] And what can we do for you, Mr Posky? I'm sorry I cant offer you a chair. That one isnt safe.

COMMISSAR. Pray dont mention it. My business will take only a moment. As you know, the Soviet Government has gone as far as possible in agreeing not to countenance or subsidize any propaganda of Communism which takes the form of a political conspiracy to overthrow the British National Government.

BISHOP. And in violation of that agreement you have corrupted my footman and changed him from an honest and respectable young Englishman into a Cell.

COMMISSAR. Have we? I know nothing of your footman. If he is intelligent enough to become a Communist, as so many famous Englishmen did long before the Russian revolution, we cannot prevent him. But we do not employ him as our agent nor support him financially in any way.

HE. But what, then, is your difficulty, Comrade Posky?

COMMISSAR. We have just discovered that there is a most dangerous organization at work in Russia, financed from the British Isles, having for its object the overthrow of the Soviet system and the substitution of the Church of England and the British Constitution.

BISHOP. And why not, sir? Why not? Could any object be more desirable, more natural? Would you in your blind hatred of British institutions and of all liberty of thought and speech, make it a crime to advocate a system which is universally admitted to be the best and freest in the world?

COMMISSAR. We do not think so. And as the obligation to refrain from this sort of propaganda is reciprocal, you are bound by it just as we are.

HE. But what is this seditious organization you have just discovered?

COMMISSAR. It is called the Society for the Propagation of the Gospel in Foreign Parts. It has agents everywhere. They call themselves missionaries.

BISHOP. I cannot bear this: the man is insane. I subscribe to the Society almost beyond my means. It is a body of the highest respectability and piety.

COMMISSAR. You are misinformed: its doctrines are of the most subversive kind. They have penetrated to my own household. My wife is a busy professional woman, and my time is taken up altogether by public work. We are absolutely dependent for our domestic work on our housekeeper Feodorovna Ballyboushka. We were ideally happy with this excellent woman for years. In her youth she was a udarnik, what you call a shock worker.

BISHOP. You are all shock workers in Russia now. You have seen the effect on me?

COMMISSAR. That was in the early days of the revolution, when she was young and ardent. Now she is elderly; and her retirement into domestic service suits her years and her helpful and affectionate temperament. Two months ago an extraordinary change came over her. She refused to do any work that was not immediately necessary, on the ground that the end of the world is at hand. She declared that she was in a condition which she described as "saved", and interrupted my work continually with attempts to save me. She had long fits of crying because she could not bear the thought of my wife spending eternity in hell. She accused the Soviets of being the hornets prophesied in the Book of Revelations. We were about to have her certified as insane—most reluctantly; for we loved our dear Ballyboushka—when we discovered that she had been hypnotized by this illegal Society. I warned our Secret Police, formerly known to you as the Gay Pay Ooh. They followed up the clue and arrested four missionaries.

BISHOP. And shot them. Christian martyrs! All who fall into the hands of the terrible Gay Pay Ooh are shot at once, without trial, without the ministrations of the Church. But I will have a memorial service said for them. To that extent at last I can defeat your Godless tyranny.

COMMISSAR. You are quite mistaken: they have not been shot. They will be sent back to England: that is all.

BISHOP [*passionately*] What right had you to arrest them? How dare you arrest Englishmen? How dare you persecute religion?

COMMISSAR. They have been very patiently examined by our official psychologists, who report that they can discover nothing that could reasonably be called religion in their minds. They are obsessed with tribal superstitions of the most barbarous kind. They believe in human sacrifices, in what they call the remission of sins by the shedding of blood. No man's life would be safe in Russia if such doctrines were propagated there.

BISHOP. But you dont understand. Oh, what dreadful ignorance!

COMMISSAR. Let us pass on to another point. Our

The Widow

police have found a secret document of your State Church, called the Thirty-nine Articles.

BISHOP. Secret! It is in the Prayer Book!

COMMISSAR. It is not read in church. That fact speaks for itself. Our police have found most of the articles incomprehensible; but there is one, the eighteenth, which declares that all Russians are to be held accursed. How would you like it if our chief cultural institution, endowed by our government, the Komintern, were to send its agents into England to teach that every Englishman is to be held accursed?

BISHOP. But surely, surely, you would not compare the Komintern to the Church of England!!

COMMISSAR. Comrade Bishop: the Komintern is the State Church in Russia exactly as the Church of England is the State Church in Britain.

The Bishop slides to the floor in another faint.

SHE. Oh! He's gone off again. Shall I get my thermos?

HE. I should break things to him more gently, Mr Posky. People die of shock. He maynt recover next time. In fact, he maynt recover this time.

COMMISSAR. What am I to do? I have said nothing that could possibly shock any educated reasonable person; but this man does not seem to know what sort of world he is living in.

SHE. He's an English bishop, you know.

COMMISSAR. Well? Is he not a rational human being?

SHE. Oh no: nothing as common as that. I tell you he's a bishop.

BISHOP. Where am I? Why am I lying on the floor? What has happened?

27

HE. You are in the Intellectual Co-operation Bureau in Geneva; and you have just been told that the Russian Komintern is analogous to the Church of England.

BISHOP [*springing to his feet unaided, his eyes blazing*] I still have life enough left in me to deny it. Karl Marx—Antichrist—said that the sweet and ennobling consolations of our faith are opium given to the poor to enable them to endure the hardships of that state of life to which it has pleased God to call them. Does your Komintern teach that blasphemy or does it not?

COMMISSAR. Impossible. There are no poor in Russia.

BISHOP. Oh! [*he drops dead*].

HE [*feeling his pulse*] I am afraid you have shocked him once too often, Comrade. His pulse has stopped. He is dead.

POSKY. Was he ever alive? To me he was incredible.

SHE. I suppose my thermos is of no use now. Shall I ring up a doctor?

HE. I think you had better ring up the police. But I say, Mr Posky, what a scoop!

COMMISSAR. A scoop? I do not understand. What is a scoop?

HE. Read all the European papers tomorrow and youll see.

ACT II

Office of the secretary of the League of Nations. Except for the small writing table at which the secretary is seated there is no office furniture. The walls are covered with engraved prints or enlarged photographs of kings, presidents, and dictators, mostly in military uniforms. Above these bellicose pictures the cornice is decorated with a row of plaster doves in low relief. There is one large picture in oils, representing a lifesize Peace, with tiny figures, also in military uniforms, kneeling round her feet and bowing their heads piously beneath the wreath which she offers them. This picture faces the secretary from the other side of the room as he sits at his table with his back to the win-

dow presenting his left profile to anyone entering from the door, which is in the middle of the wall between them. A suite of half a dozen chairs is ranged round the walls, except one, which stands near the writing table for the convenience of people interviewing the secretary.

He is a disillusioned official with a habit of dogged patience acquired in the course of interviews with distinguished statesmen of different nations, all in a condition of invincible ignorance as to the spirit of Geneva and the constitution of the League of Nations, and each with a national axe to grind. On this occasion he is rather exceptionally careworn. One pities him, as he is of a refined type, and, one guesses, began as a Genevan idealist. Age fifty or thereabouts.

There is a telephone on the table which he is at present using.

THE SECRETARY. Yes: send her up instantly. Remind me of her name. What?! . . . Ammonia? Nonsense! that cant be her name. Spell it . . . V E? . . . Oh, *B* E. Do you mean to say that her name is Begonia? Begonia Brown? . . . Farcical.

He replaces the receiver as Begonia enters. She is the Intellectual Co-operation typist. She is in walking dress, cheap, but very smart.

THE SECRETARY. Miss Brown?

BEGONIA [*with her best smile*] Yes.

THE SECRETARY. Sit down.

BEGONIA [*complying*] Kew [*short for Thank you*].

THE SECRETARY [*gravely*] You have heard the news, no doubt?

BEGONIA. Oh yes. Jack Palamedes has won the

dancing tournament. I had ten francs on him; and I
have won a hundred. Had you anything on?

THE SECRETARY [*still more gravely*] I am afraid you
will think me very ignorant, Miss Brown; but I have
never heard of Mr Palamedes.

BEGONIA. Fancy that! He's the talk of Geneva, I
assure you.

THE SECRETARY. There are other items of news,
Miss Brown. Germany has withdrawn from the
League.

BEGONIA. And a good riddance, if you ask me. My
father lost a lot of money through the war. Otherwise
—you wont mind my telling you—youd never have
got me slaving at a typewriter here for my living.

THE SECRETARY. No doubt. A further item is that
the British Empire has declared war on Russia.

BEGONIA. Well, what could you expect us to do
with those awful Bolshies? We should have done it
long ago. But thank goodness we're safe in Geneva,
you and I.

THE SECRETARY. We are safe enough everywhere,
so far. The war is one of sanctions only.

BEGONIA. More shame for us, say I. I should give
those Bolshies the bayonet: thats the way to talk to
scum of that sort. I cant contain myself when I think
of all the murder and slavery of them Soviets—[*correcting herself*] those Soviets.

THE SECRETARY. In consequence Japan has declared
war on Russia and is therefore in military alliance
with Britain. And the result of that is that Australia,
New Zealand and Canada have repudiated the war
and formed an anti-Japanese alliance with the United

States under the title of the New British Federation.
South Africa may join them at any moment.

BEGONIA [*flushing with indignation*] Do you mean
that theyve broken up our dear Empire?

THE SECRETARY. They have said nothing about that.

BEGONIA. Oh, then thats quite all right. You know,
when I was at school I was chosen five times to recite on
Empire Day; and in my very first year, when I was the
smallest child there, I presented the bouquet to King
George's sister, who came to our prize giving. Say a
word against the Empire, and you have finished with
Begonia Brown.

THE SECRETARY. Then you went to school, did you?

BEGONIA. Well, of course: what do you take me
for? I went to school for seven years and never missed a
single day. I got fourteen prizes for regular attendance.

THE SECRETARY. Good God!

BEGONIA. What did you say?

THE SECRETARY. Nothing. I was about to tell you
what has happened in Quetzalcopolis, the chief seaport of the Earthly Paradise.

BEGONIA. I know. In Central America, isnt it?

THE SECRETARY. Yes. The mob there has attacked
the British Consulate, and torn down the British flag.

BEGONIA [*rising in a fury*] Insulted the British
flag!!!

THE SECRETARY. They have also burnt down three
convents and two churches.

BEGONIA. Thats nothing: theyre only Catholic
churches. But do you mean to say that they have dared
to touch the British flag?

THE SECRETARY. They have. Fortunately it was

32

after hours and the staff had gone home. Otherwise they would assuredly have been massacred.

BEGONIA. Dirty swine! I hope the British fleet will not leave a stone standing or a nigger alive in their beastly seaport. Thatll teach them.

THE SECRETARY. There is only one other trifle of news. The little Dominion of Jacksonland has declared itself an independent republic.

BEGONIA. It ought to be ashamed of itself. Republics are a low lot. But dont you be anxious about that: the republicans will soon be kicked out. The people may be misled for awhile; but they always come back to king and country.

THE SECRETARY. And now, Miss Brown, I must ask you whether you fully realize that all this is your doing?

BEGONIA. Mine!

THE SECRETARY. Yours and nobody else's. In every one of these cases, it was your hand that started the series of political convulsions which may end in the destruction of civilization.

BEGONIA [*flattered*] Really? How?

THE SECRETARY. Those letters that you sent to the Court of International Justice at the Hague—

BEGONIA. Oh, of course. Yes. Fancy that!

THE SECRETARY. But did you not know what you were doing? You conducted the correspondence with very remarkable ability—more, I confess, than I should have given you credit for. Do you mean to tell me that you did not foresee the consequences of your action? That you did not even read the newspapers to see what was happening?

BEGONIA. I dont read political news: it's so dry. However, I seem to be having a big success; and I wont pretend I am not gratified.

THE SECRETARY. Unfortunately the Powers do not consider it a success. They are blaming me for it.

BEGONIA. Oh, if there is any blame I am ready to take it all on myself.

THE SECRETARY. That is very magnanimous of you, Miss Brown.

BEGONIA. Not so magnanimous either: thank you all the same. I tell you I back the Empire; and the Empire will back me. So dont be uneasy.

THE SECRETARY. You are very possibly right. And now may I ask you a personal question? How did you become interested in the League of Nations? How did you get this post of yours, which has placed the world's destiny so unexpectedly in your hands?

BEGONIA. Was I interested in the League? Let me see. You know that there is a Society called the League of Nations Union, dont you?

THE SECRETARY. I do. I shudder whenever I think of it.

BEGONIA. Oh, theres no harm in it. I'd never heard of it until last year, when they opened a branch in

The Journalist

Camberwell with a whist drive. A friend gave me a
ticket for it. It was opened by the Conservative candidate: an innocent young lad rolling in money. He
saw that I was a cut above the other girls there, and
picked me for his partner when he had to dance. I told
him I'd won a County Council scholarship and was
educated and knew shorthand and a bit of French and
all that, and that I was looking out for a job. His
people fixed me up for Geneva all right. A perfect
gentleman I must say: never asked so much as a kiss.
I was disappointed.

THE SECRETARY. Disappointed at his not kissing
you?

BEGONIA. Oh no: there were plenty of kisses going
from better looking chaps. But he was a bit of a sucker;
and I thought he had intentions; and of course he
would have been a jolly good catch for me. But when
his people got wind of it they packed him off for a tour
round the Empire, and got me this job here—to keep
me out of his way, I suppose. Anyhow here I am, you
see.

THE SECRETARY. Were you examined as to your
knowledge and understanding of the Covenant of the
League, and its constitution?

BEGONIA. No. They didnt need to examine me to
find out that I was educated. I had lots of prizes and
certificates; and there was my L.C.C. scholarship.
You see, I have such a good memory: examinations
are no trouble to me. Theres a book in the office about
the League. I tried to read it; but it was such dry stuff
I went to sleep over it.

THE SECRETARY [rising] Well, Miss Brown, I am

glad to have made your acquaintance, and delighted to learn that though you have produced a first class political crisis, including what promises to be a world war, and made an amazing change in the constitution of the British Empire all in the course of a single morning's work, you are still in high spirits and in fact rather proud of yourself.

BEGONIA [*she has also risen*] Oh, I am not a bit proud; and I'm quite used to being a success. You know, although I was always at the top of my class at school, I never pretended to be clever. Silly clever, I call it. At first I was frightened of the girls that went in for being clever and having original ideas and all that sort of crankiness. But I beat them easily in the examinations; and they never got anywhere. That gave me confidence. Wherever I go I always find that

lots of people think as I do. The best sort of people always do: the real ladies and gentlemen, you know. The others are oddities and outsiders. If you want to know what real English public opinion is, keep your eye on me. I'm not a bit afraid of war: remember that England has never lost a battle, and that it does no harm to remind the foreigners of it when they get out of hand. Good morning. So pleased to have met you.

They shake hands; and he goes to the door and opens it for her. She goes out much pleased with herself.

THE SECRETARY [*ruminating dazedly*] And thats England! [*The telephone rings. He returns to the table to attend to it*]. Yes? . . . Which Foreign Secretary? Every hole and corner in the Empire has its own Foreign Secretary now. Do you mean the British Foreign Secretary, Sir Orpheus Midlander? . . . Well, why didnt you say so? Shew him up at once.

Sir Orpheus comes in. He is a very welldressed gentleman of fifty or thereabouts, genial in manner, quickwitted in conversation, altogether a pleasant and popular personality.

THE SECRETARY. Do sit down. I cant say how I feel about your being dragged here all the way from London in Derby week.

SIR O. [*sitting*] Well, my friend, it's you who have dragged me. And I hope you wont mind my asking you what on earth you think you have been doing? What induced you to do it?

THE SECRETARY. I didnt do it. It was done by the Committee for Intellectual Co-operation.

SIR O. The what??! I never heard of such a body.

THE SECRETARY. Neither did I until this business was sprung on me. Nobody ever heard of it. But I find now that it is part of the League, and that its members are tremendous swells with European reputations. Theyve all published translations from the Greek or discovered new planets or something of that sort.

SIR O. Ah yes: outside politics: I see. But we cant have literary people interfering in foreign affairs. And

37

they must have held meetings before taking such an outrageous step as this. Why were we not told? We'd have squashed them at once.

THE SECRETARY. They are quite innocent: they know no more about it than I did. The whole thing was done by a young woman named Begonia Brown.

SIR O. Begonia Brown! But this is appalling. I shall be personally compromised.

THE SECRETARY. You! How?

SIR O. This woman—it must be the same woman; for there cant be another female with such a name in the world—she's engaged to my nephew.

THE SECRETARY. She told me about it. But I had no idea the man was your nephew. I see how awkward it is for you. Did you ever talk to her about it?

SIR O. I! I never set eyes on her in my life. I remember her ridiculous name: thats all.

THE SECRETARY. Were you in the habit of discussing foreign affairs with your nephew?

SIR O. With Benjy! You might as well discuss Einstein's general theory of relativity with a blue behinded ape. I havnt exchanged twenty words with the boy since I tipped him when he was going from Eton to Oxford.

THE SECRETARY. Then I cant understand it. Her correspondence with the Hague Court has been conducted with remarkable ability and in first-rate style. The woman herself is quite incapable of it. There must be somebody behind her. Can it be your nephew?

SIR O. If, as you say, the work shews political ability and presentable style, you may accept my assurance that Sue's boy has nothing to do with it. Besides, he is at present in Singapore, where the native dancing girls are irresistible.

The telephone rings.

THE SECRETARY. Excuse me. Yes? . . . Hold on a moment. [*To Sir O.*] The Senior Judge of the Court of International Justice at the Hague is downstairs. Hadnt you better see him?

SIR O. By all means. Most opportune.

THE SECRETARY [*into the telephone*] Send him up.

SIR O. Have you had any correspondence about this business?

THE SECRETARY. Correspondence!!! I havnt read one tenth of it. The Abyssinian war was a holiday job in comparison. Weve never had anything like it before.

The Senior Judge enters. He is a Dutchman, much younger than a British judge: under forty, in fact, but very grave and every inch a judge.

THE SECRETARY. I am desolate at having brought your honor all the way from the Hague. A word from you would have brought me there and saved you the trouble. Have you met the British Foreign Secretary, Sir Orpheus Midlander?

JUDGE. I have not had that pleasure. How do you do, Sir Midlander?

SIR O. How do you do?

They shake hands whilst the Secretary places a chair for the judge in the middle of the room, between his table and Sir Orpheus. They all sit down.

JUDGE. I thought it best to come. The extraordinary feature of this affair is that I have communicated

39

with all the members of the Intellectual Committee; and every one of them denies any knowledge of it. Most of them did not know that they are members.

SIR O. Do you mean to say that it is all a hoax?

JUDGE. It may be that someone was hoaxing the Court. But now that the applications for warrants have been made public, the Court must take them seriously. Otherwise it would cut a ridiculous figure in the eyes of Europe.

SIR O. But surely such a procedure was never contemplated when the Powers joined the League?

JUDGE. I do not think anything was contemplated when the Powers joined the League. They signed the Covenant without reading it, to oblige President Wilson. The United States then refused to sign it to disoblige President Wilson, also without reading it. Since then the Powers have behaved in every respect as if the League did not exist, except when they could use it for their own purposes.

SIR O. [naïvely] But how else could they use it?

JUDGE. They could use it to maintain justice and order between the nations.

SIR O. There is nothing we desire more. The British Empire stands for justice and order. But I must tell you that the British Foreign Office would take a very grave view of any attempt on the part of the Court to do anything without consulting us. I need not remind you that without us you have no powers. You have no police to execute your warrants. You cant put the Powers in the dock: you havnt got a dock.

JUDGE. We have a court room at the Hague which can easily be provided with a dock if you consider

The Bishop

such a construction necessary, which I do not. We have employees to whom we can assign police duties to any necessary extent.

SIR O. Pooh! You cant be serious. You have no jurisdiction.

JUDGE. You mean that our jurisdiction is undefined. That means that our jurisdiction is what we choose to make it. You are familiar with what you call judgemade law in England. Well, Sir Midlander, the judges of the Court of International Justice are not nonentities. We have waited a long time for a case to set us in motion. You have provided us with four cases; and you may depend on us to make the most of them. They will affirm our existence, which is hardly known yet. They will exercise our power, which is hardly felt yet. All we needed was a *cause célèbre*; and Miss Begonia has found several for us very opportunely.

SIR O. My dear sir: Miss Brown is a nobody.

JUDGE. Unless the highest court can be set in motion by the humblest individual justice is a mockery.

SIR O. Of course I agree with that—in principle. Still, you know, there are people you can take into court and people you cant. Your experience at the bar—

JUDGE [*interrupting him sharply*] I have had no experience at the bar. Please remember that you are not now in England, where judges are only worn-out barristers, most of whom have forgotten any sense of law they may ever have acquired.

SIR O. How very odd! I own I was surprised to

41

find the judicial bench represented by so young a man; and I am afraid I must add that I prefer our British system. We should have had no trouble with a British judge.

JUDGE. Why should you have any trouble with me? I am simply a Judge, first and last. To me it is a continual trouble and scandal that modern statesmen are slipping back, one after another, from the reign of law based on the eternal principle of justice, to the maintenance of governments set up by successful demagogues or victorious soldiers, each of whom has his proscription list of enemies whom he imprisons, exiles, or murders at his pleasure until he is himself overcome by an abler rival and duly proscribed, imprisoned, exiled or assassinated in his turn. Such a state of things is abhorrent to me. I have spent years in trying to devise some judicial procedure by which these law-breakers can be brought to justice. Well, the

Intellectual Co-operation Committee—of the existence of which I must confess I was entirely ignorant— has found the procedure; and the Court will back it up to the utmost of its powers.

SIR O. I am afraid you are a bit of an idealist.

JUDGE. Necessarily. Justice is an ideal; and I am a judge. What, may I ask, are you?

SIR O. I! Oh, only a much harassed Foreign Secretary. You see, my young friend—if you will allow me to call you so—justice, as you say, is an ideal, and a very fine ideal too; but what I have to deal with is Power; and Power is often a devilishly ugly thing. If any of these demagogue dictators issues a warrant for your arrest or even an order for your execution, you will be arrested and shot the moment you set foot in their country. You may even be kidnapped and carried there: remember Napoleon and the Duc d'Enghien. But if you issue a warrant or pronounce a sentence against one of them Europe will just laugh at you, because you have no power. It will be as futile as a decree of excommunication.

JUDGE. Would you like to be excommunicated?

SIR O. Hardly a serious question, is it?

JUDGE. Very serious.

SIR O. My dear sir, it couldnt happen.

JUDGE. Pardon me: it could.

SIR O. [*obstinately*] Pardon me: it couldnt. Look at the thing practically. To begin with I am not a Roman Catholic. I am a member of the Church of England; and down at my place in the country the Church living is in my gift. Without my subscription the churchwardens could not make both ends meet. The rector has no society except what he gets in my house.

JUDGE. The rector is a freeholder. If you are a notoriously evil liver, he can refuse to admit you to Communion.

SIR O. But I am not a notoriously evil liver. If the rector suggested such a thing I should have him out

43

of his rectory and in a lunatic asylum before the end of the week.

JUDGE. Suppose the rector were prepared to risk that! Suppose the war of 1914 were renewed, and you were responsible for sending the young men of your country to drop bombs on the capital cities of Europe! Suppose your rector, as a Christian priest, took the view that you were in a condition of mortal sin and refused you Communion! Suppose, if you wish, that you had him locked up as a lunatic! Would you like it?

SIR O. Suppose the villagers burnt down his rectory and ducked him in the horse pond to teach him a little British patriotism! How would he like it?

JUDGE. Martyrdom has its attractions for some natures. But my question was not whether he would like it, but whether you would like it.

SIR O. I should treat it with contempt.

JUDGE. No doubt; but would you like it?

SIR O. Oh, come! Really! Really!

JUDGE. Believe me, Sir Midlander, you would not like it. And if the International Court, moved by the Committee for Intellectual Co-operation, were to deliver an adverse judgment on you, you would not like it. The man whom the Hague condemns will be an uncomfortable man. The State which it finds to be in the wrong will be an uncomfortable State.

SIR O. But you cant enforce anything. You have no sanctions.

JUDGE. What, exactly, do you mean by sanctions, Sir Midlander?

SIR O. I mean what everybody means. Sanctions, you know. That is plain English. Oil, for instance.

JUDGE. Castor oil?

SIR O. No no: motor oil. The stuff you run your aeroplanes on.

JUDGE. Motor oil is a sanction when you withhold it. Castor oil is a sanction when you administer it. Is there any other difference?

SIR O. [*smiling*] Well, that has never occurred to me before; but now you mention it there is certainly an analogy. But in England the castor oil business is just one of those things that are not done. Castor oil is indecent. Motor oil is all right.

JUDGE. Well, you need not fear that the Hague will resort to any other sanction than the sacredness of justice. It will affirm this sacredness and make the necessary applications. It is the business of a judge to see that there is no wrong without a remedy. Your Committee for Intellectual Co-operation has been appealed to by four persons who have suffered grievous wrongs. It has very properly referred them to the International Court. As president of that court it is my business to find a remedy for their wrongs; and I shall do so to the best of my ability even if my decisions should form the beginning of a new code of international law and be quite unprecedented.

SIR O. But, my dear sir, what practical steps do you propose to take? What steps can you take?

D

JUDGE. I have already taken them. I have fixed a day for the trial of the cases, and summoned the plaintiffs and defendants to attend the court.

THE SECRETARY. But the defendants are the responsible heads of sovereign States. Do you suppose for a moment that they will obey your summons?

JUDGE. We shall see. That, in fact, is the object of my experiment. We shall see. [*He rises*] And now I must ask you to excuse me. Sir Midlander: our interview has been most instructive to me as to the attitude of your country. Mr Secretary: you are very good to have spared me so much of your valuable time. Good afternoon, gentlemen. [*He goes out*].

SIR O. What are we to do with men like that?

THE SECRETARY. What are they going to do with us? That is the question we have to face now.

SIR O. Pooh! They cant do anything, you know, except make speeches and write articles. They are free to do that in England. British liberty is a most useful safety valve.

THE SECRETARY. I was on his honor's side myself once, until my official experience here taught me how hopeless it is to knock supernationalism—

SIR O. Super what? Did you say supernaturalism?

THE SECRETARY. No Supernationalism.

SIR O. Oh, I see. Internationalism.

THE SECRETARY. No Internationalism is nonsense. Pushing all the nations into Geneva is like throwing all the fishes into the same pond: they just begin eating oneanother. We need something higher than nationalism: a genuine political and social catholicism. How are you to get that from these patriots, with their

Commissar Poshy

national anthems and flags and dreams of war and conquest rubbed into them from their childhood? The organization of nations is the organization of world war. If two men want to fight how do you prevent them? By keeping them apart, not by bringing them together. When the nations kept apart war was an occasional and exceptional thing: now the League hangs over Europe like a perpetual war-cloud.

SIR O. Well, dont throw it at my head as if I disagreed with you.

THE SECRETARY. I beg your pardon. I am worried by this crisis. Let us talk business. What are we to do with Begonia Brown?

SIR O. Do with her! Squash her, impudent little slut. She is nobody: she doesnt matter.

The conversation is abruptly broken by the irruption of Begonia herself in a state of ungovernable excitement.

BEGONIA. Have you heard the news? [*Seeing Sir Orpheus*] Oh, I beg your pardon: I didnt know you were engaged.

THE SECRETARY. This is Sir Orpheus Midlander, the British Foreign Secretary, Miss Brown.

BEGONIA. Oh, most pleased to meet you, Sir Orpheus. I know your nephew. We are quite dear friends [*she shakes Sir O.'s hand effusively*]. Have you heard the news? Lord Middlesex is dead.

SIR O. Indeed? Let me see. Middlesex? I dont attach any significance to the news. He must have been a backwoodsman. Remind me about him.

BEGONIA. His son is Lord Newcross.

SIR O. Oh! Then Newcross goes to the Lords to

succeed his father. That means a by-election in Camberwell.

BEGONIA. Yes; and the Conservatives want me to stand.

BOTH GENTLEMEN. What!!!

BEGONIA. Dont you think I ought to? I have been a lot in the papers lately. It's six hundred a year for me if I get in. I shall be the patriotic candidate; and the Labor vote will be a split vote; for the Communists are putting up a candidate against the Labor man; and the Liberals are contesting the seat as well. It will be just a walk-over for me.

SIR O. But my nephew is the Government candidate. Has he not told you so?

BEGONIA. Oh, thats quite all right. He has withdrawn and proposed me. He'll pay my election expenses.

SIR O. I thought he was in Singapore.

BEGONIA. So he is. It's all been done by cable. Ive just this minute heard it. You see, dear Billikins is not very bright; and he'd better not be here to muddle everything up. [*She sits*].

SIR O. But will his committee accept you?

BEGONIA. Only too glad to get a candidate that will do them credit. You see, no matter how carefully they coached Bill for the public meetings he made the most awful exhibition of himself. And he knew it, poor lamb, and would never have gone in for it if his mother hadnt made him.

SIR O. And do you think you will be able to make a better impression at the meetings? You are not a politician, are you?

48

BEGONIA. The same as anybody else, I suppose. I shall pick up all the politics I need when I get into the House; and I shall get into the House because there are lots of people in Camberwell who think as I do. You bet I shall romp in at the head of the poll. I am quite excited about it. [*To the Secretary*] You were so kind to me just now that I thought you had a right to know before anyone else. [*To Sir O.*] And it's splendid news for the Government, isnt it, Sir Orpheus?

SIR O. Thrilling, Miss Brown.

BEGONIA. Oh, do call me Begonia. We're as good as related, arnt we?

SIR O. I am afraid so.

BEGONIA. I am sure to get in, arnt I?

SIR O. If your three oppo-nents are foolish enough to go to the poll, it's a cert.

BEGONIA. Yes: isnt it? I wonder would you mind lend-ing me my fare to London. I dont like taking money off Billikins. I will pay you when my ship comes home: the six hundred a year, you know.

SIR O. Will a five pound note be any use [*he produces one*]?

BEGONIA [*taking it*] Thanks ever so much: itll just see me through. And now I must toddle off to my little constituency. I have barely time to pack for the night train. Goodbye, Mr Secretary

[*They shake hands*]; and [*to Sir O. effusively*] thanks ever so much, and au revoir. [*She goes out*].

THE SECRETARY. What an amazing young woman! You really think she will get in?

SIR O. Of course she will. She has courage, sincerity, good looks, and big publicity as the Geneva heroine. Everything that our voters love.

THE SECRETARY. But she hasnt a political idea in her head.

SIR O. She need not have. The Whips will pilot her through the division lobby until she knows the way. She need not know anything else.

THE SECRETARY. But she is a complete ignoramus. She will give herself away every time she opens her mouth.

SIR O. Not at all. She will say pluckily and sincerely just what she feels and thinks. You heard her say that there are lots of people in Camberwell who feel and think as she does. Well, the House of Commons is exactly like Camberwell in that respect.

THE SECRETARY. But can you contemplate such a state of things without dismay?

SIR O. Of course I can. I contemplated my nephew's candidature without dismay.

THE SECRETARY. The world is mad. Quite mad.

SIR O. Pooh! you need a cup of tea. Nothing wrong with the world: nothing whatever.

THE SECRETARY [*resignedly sitting down and speaking into the telephone*] Tea for two, please.

ACT III

*A salon in the old palace of the Hague. On a spacious
dais a chair of State, which is in fact an old throne, is at
the head of a table furnished with chairs, writing mater-
ials, and buttons connected with telephonic apparatus.
The table occupies the centre of the dais. On the floor at
both sides chairs are arranged in rows for the accomoda-
tion of spectators, litigants, witnesses, &c. The tall win-
dows admit abundance of sunlight and shew up all the*

gilding and grandeur of the immovables. The door is at the side, on the right of the occupant of the chair of state, at present empty. The formal arrangement of the furniture suggests a sitting or hearing or meeting of some kind. A waste paper basket is available.

The Secretary of the League of Nations has a little central table to himself in front of the other. His profile points towards the door. Behind him, in the front row of chairs are the Jew, the Commissar and the Widow. In the opposite front row are Begonia and a cheerful young gentleman, powerfully built, with an uproarious voice which he subdues to conversational pitch with some difficulty. Next him is the quondam Newcomer. They are all reading newspapers. Begonia and her young man have one excessively illustrated newspaper between them. He has his arm round her waist and is shamelessly enjoying their physical contact. The two are evidently betrothed.

THE JEW. Do you think anything is really going to happen, Mr Secretary?

THE SECRETARY. Possibly not. I am here to be able to report from personal knowledge whether any notice has been taken of the summonses issued by the court.

THE BETROTHED. The judge himself hasnt turned up.

THE SECRETARY (*looking at his watch*). He is not due yet: you have all come too early.

THE BETROTHED. We came early to make sure of getting seats. And theres not a soul in the bally place except ourselves.

Sir Orpheus comes in.

The Secretary

SIR ORPHEUS. What! Nobody but ourselves! Dont they admit the public?

THE SECRETARY. The public is not interested, it seems.

BEGONIA. One free lance journalist looked in; but she went away when she found there was nothing doing.

THE BETROTHED. The doors are open all right. All are affectionately invited.

SIR ORPHEUS (*seating himself next Begonia*). But what a dreadful fiasco for our friend the judge! I warned him that this might happen. I told him to send special invitations to the press, and cards to all the leading people and foreign visitors. And here! not a soul except ourselves! All Europe will laugh at him.

THE SECRETARY. Yes; but if the affair is going to be a fiasco the fewer people there are to witness it the better.

BEGONIA. After all, theres more than half a dozen of us. Quite a distinguished audience I call it. Remember, you are the Foreign Secretary, Nunky. You are an honorable, Billikins. And I'm not exactly a nobody.

THE BETROTHED (*kissing her hand*) My ownest and bestest, you are a Dame of the British Empire. The Camberwell Times has celebrated your birthday by a poem hailing you as the Lily of Geneva; but on this occasion only, you are not the centre of European interest. The stupendous and colossal joke of the present proceedings is that this court has summoned all the dictators to appear before it and answer charges brought against them by the Toms, Dicks, Harriets, Susans and Elizas of all nations.

THE WIDOW. Pardon me, young Señor. I am neither Susan nor Eliza.

THE BETROTHED. Present company excepted, of course, Señora. But the point—the staggering, paralyzing, jolly bally breath-bereaving point of our assembly today is that the dictators have been summoned and that they wont come. Young Johnny Judge has no more authority over them than his cat.

THE NEWCOMER. But if they wont come, gentlemen, what are we here for?

THE BETROTHED. To see the fun when Johnny Judge comes and finds nothing doing, I suppose.

THE WIDOW. Is he not late? We seem to have been waiting here for ages.

THE SECRETARY [*looking at his watch*] He is due now. It is on the stroke of ten.

The Judge, in his judicial robe, enters. They all rise. He is in high spirits and very genial.

THE JUDGE [*shaking hands with Sir Orpheus*] Good morning, Sir Midlander. [*He passes on to the judicial chair, greeting them as he goes*] Good morning, ladies and gentlemen. Good morning, mademoiselle. Good morning, Señora. Good morning. Good morning. [*Takes his seat*] Pray be seated.

They all sit, having bowed speechlessly to his salutations.

THE JUDGE. Any defendants yet, Mr Secretary?

THE SECRETARY. None, your Honor. The parties on your left are all plaintiffs. On your right, Sir Orpheus Midlander has a watching brief for the British Foreign Office. The lady, Dame Begonia Brown, represents the Committee for Intellectual

54

Co-operation. The young gentleman is the public.

THE JUDGE. An impartial spectator, eh?

THE BETROTHED. No, my lord. Very partial to the girl. Engaged, in fact.

THE JUDGE. My best congratulations. May I warn you all that the instruments on the table are microphones and televisors? I have arranged so as to avoid a crowd and make our proceedings as unconstrained and comfortable as possible; but our apparent privacy is quite imaginary.

General consternation. They all sit up as in church.

BEGONIA. But they should have told us this when we came in. Billikins has been sitting with his arm round my waist, whispering all sorts of silly things. Theyll be in The Camberwell Times tomorrow.

THE JUDGE. I'm sorry. You should have been warned. In the International Court no walls can hide you, and no distance deaden your lightest whisper. We are all seen and heard in Rome, in Moscow, in London, wherever the latest type of receiver is installed.

BEGONIA. Heard! You mean overheard.

THE WIDOW. And overlooked. Our very clothes are transparent to the newest rays. It is scandalous.

THE JUDGE. Not at all, Señora. The knowledge that we all live in public, and that there are no longer any secret places where evil things can be done and wicked conspiracies discussed, may produce a great improvement in morals.

THE WIDOW. I protest. All things that are private are not evil; but they may be extremely indecent.

BEGONIA. We'd better change the subject, I think

THE BETROTHED. What about the dictators, my lord? Do you really think any of them will come?

THE JUDGE. They are not under any physical compulsion to come. But every day of their lives they do things they are not physically compelled to do.

SIR ORPHEUS. That is a fact, certainly. But it is hardly a parliamentary fact.

A telephone rings on the Judge's desk. He holds down a button and listens.

THE JUDGE. You will not have to wait any longer, Sir Midlander. [*Into the telephone*] We are waiting for him. Shew him the way. [*He releases the button*]. The very first dictator to arrive is Signor Bombardone.

ALL THE REST. Bombardone!!!

The Dictator enters, dominant, brusque, every inch a man of destiny.

BOMBARDONE. Is this the so-called International Court?

THE JUDGE. It is.

BOMBARDONE. My name is Bombardone. [*He mounts the dais; takes the nearest chair with a powerful hand and places it on the Judge's left; then flings himself massively into it*] Do not let my presence embarrass you. Proceed.

THE JUDGE. I have to thank you, Signor Bombardone, for so promptly obeying the summons of the court.

BOMBARDONE. I obey nothing. I am here because it is my will to be here. My will is part of the world's will. A large part, as it happens. The world moves towards internationalism. Without this movement to nerve you you would never have had the audacity to summon me. Your action is therefore a symptom of the movement of civilization. Wherever such a symptom can be detected I have a place: a leading place.

SIR ORPHEUS. But pardon me, Signor: I understand that you are a great nationalist. How can you be at once a nationalist and an internationalist?

BOMBARDONE. How can I be anything else? How do you build a house? By first making good sound bricks. You cant build it of mud. The nations are the bricks out of which the future world State must be built. I consolidated my country as a nation: a white nation. I then added a black nation to it and made it an empire. When the empires federate, its leaders will govern the world; and these leaders will have a superleader who will be the ablest man in the world: that is my vision. I leave you to imagine what I think of the mob of bagmen from fifty potty little foreign States that calls itself a League of Nations.

JUDGE. Your country is a member of that League, Signor.

BOMBARDONE. My country has to keep an eye on fools. The scripture tells us that it is better to meet a bear in our path than a fool. Fools are dangerous; and the so-called League of Nations is a League of Fools; therefore the wise must join it to watch them. That is why all the effective Powers are in the League, as well as the little toy republics we shall swallow up in due time.

THE ÇI-DEVANT NEWCOMER. Steady on, mister. I dont understand.

BOMBARDONE [contemptuously to the Judge] Tell him that this is a court of people who understand, and that the place of those who do not understand is in the ranks of silent and blindly obedient labor.

NEWCOMER. Oh, thats your game, is it? Who are you that I should obey you? What about democracy?

BOMBARDONE. I am what I am: you are what you are; and in virtue of these two facts I am where I am and you are where you are. Try to change places with me: you may as well try to change the path of the sun through the heavens.

THE NEWCOMER. You think a lot of yourself, dont you? I ask you again: what about democracy?

An unsmiling middle aged gentleman with slim figure, erect carriage, and resolutely dissatisfied expression, wanders in.

THE DISSATISFIED GENTLEMAN. Is this the sitting of the department of international justice?

Feliks Topolski

Liz Orpheus Midlander

BOMBARDONE [*springing up*] Battler, by all thats unexpected!

BATTLER [*equally surprised*] Bombardone, by all thats underhand!

BOMBARDONE. You thought you could steal a march on me, eh?

BATTLER. You have ambushed me. Fox!

BOMBARDONE [*sitting down*] Undignified, Ernest. Undignified.

BATTLER. True, Bardo. I apologize. [*He takes a chair from behind Sir Orpheus, and mounts the dais to the right of the Judge, who now has a dictator on each side of him*] By your leave, sir. [*He sits*].

JUDGE. I thank you, Mr Battler, for obeying the summons of the court.

BATTLER. Obedience is hardly the word, sir.

JUDGE. You have obeyed. You are here. Why?

BATTLER. That is just what I have come to find out. Why are you here, Bardo?

BOMBARDONE. I am everywhere.

THE BETROTHED [*boisterously*] Ha ha! Ha ha ha! Dam funny, that.

THE JUDGE. I must ask the public not to smile.

NEWCOMER [*who has no sense of humor*] Smile! He was not smiling: he laughed right out. With all respect to your worship we are wasting our time talking nonsense. How can a man be everywhere? The other gentleman says he came here to find out why he came here. It isnt sense. These two gents are balmy.

BOMBARDONE. Pardon me. What does balmy mean?

NEWCOMER. Balmy. Off your chumps. If you want it straight, mad.

59

BOMBARDONE. You belong to the lower orders, I see.

NEWCOMER. Who are you calling lower orders? Dont you know that democracy has put an end to all that?

BOMBARDONE. On the contrary, my friend, democracy has given a real meaning to it for the first time. Democracy has thrown us both into the same pair of scales. Your pan has gone up: mine has gone down; and nothing will bring down your pan while I am sitting in the other. Democracy has delivered you from the law of priest and king, of landlord and capitalist, only to bring you under the law of personal gravitation. Personal gravitation is a law of nature. You cannot cut its head off.

NEWCOMER. Democracy can cut your head off. British democracy has cut off thicker heads before.

BOMBARDONE. Never. Plutocracy has cut off the heads of kings and archbishops to make itself supreme and rob the people without interference from king or priest; but the people always follow their born leader. When there is no leader, no king, no priest, nor any body of law established by dead kings and priests, you have mob law, lynching law, gangster law: in short, American democracy. Thank your stars you have never known democracy in England. I have rescued my country from all that by my leadership. I am a democratic institution.

NEWCOMER. Gosh. You democratic! Youve abolished democracy, you have.

BOMBARDONE. Put my leadership to the vote. Take a plebiscite. If I poll less than 95 per cent of the adult nation I will resign. If that is not democracy what is democracy?

NEWCOMER. It isnt British democracy.

BATTLER. British democracy is a lie. I have said it.

NEWCOMER. Oh, dont talk nonsense, you ignorant foreigner. Plebiscites are unEnglish, thoroughly un-English.

BEGONIA. Hear hear!

SIR O. May I venture to make an observation?

BATTLER. Who are you?

SIR O. Only a humble Englishman, listening most respectfully to your clever and entertaining conversation. Officially, I am the British Foreign Secretary.

Both Leaders rise and give the Fascist salute. Sir Orpheus remains seated, but waves his hand graciously.

BBDE. I must explain to the court that England is no longer of any consequence apart from me. I have dictated her policy for years [*he sits.*]

BATTLER. I have snapped my fingers in England's face on

every issue that has risen between us. Europe looks
to me, not to England. [*He also resumes his seat*].

SIR O. You attract attention, Mr Battler: you certainly do attract attention. And you, Signor Bombardone, are quite welcome to dictate our policy as
long as it is favorable to us. But the fact is, we are
mostly unconscious of these triumphs of yours in
England. I listen to your account of them with perfect
complacency and—I hope you will not mind my saying so—with some amusement. But I must warn you
that if your triumphs ever lead you to any steps contrary to the interests of the British Empire we shall
have to come down rather abruptly from triumphs to
facts; and the facts may not work so smoothly as the
triumphs.

BATTLER. What could you do, facts or no facts?

SIR O. I dont know.

BATTLER. } You dont know!!!
BOMBARDONE.

SIR O. I dont know. Nor do you, Mr Battler. Nor
you, Signor.

BBDE. Do you mean that I do not know what you
could do, or that I do not know what I should do.

SIR O. Both, Signor.

BBDE. What have you to say to that, Ernest?

BATTLER. I should know what to do: have no doubt
about that.

SIR O. You mean that you would know what to do
when you knew what England was going to do?

BATTLER. I know already what you could do. Nothing. I tore up your peace treaty and threw the pieces
in your face. You did nothing. I took your last Lo-

carno pact and marched 18,000 soldiers through it.
I threw down a frontier and doubled the size and
power of my realm in spite of your teeth. What did
you do? Nothing.

SIR O. Of course we did nothing. It did not suit us
to do anything. A child of six could have foreseen that
we should do nothing; so you shook your fist at us and
cried "Do anything if you dare." Your countrymen
thought you a hero. But as you knew you were quite
safe, we were not
impressed.

BBDE. You are
quite right, Excel-
lency. It was your
folly and France's
that blew Ernest up
the greasy pole of
political ambition.
Still, he has a flair for
power; and he has
my example to en-
courage him. Do
not despise Ernest.

BATTLER. I have never concealed my admiration for
you, Bardo. But you have a failing that may ruin you
unless you learn to keep it in check.

BBDE. And what is that, pray?

BATTLER. Selfconceit. You think yourself the only
great man in the world.

BBDE. [*calm*] Can you name a greater?

BATTLER. There are rivals in Russia, Arabia, and
Iran.

BRDB. And there is Ernest the Great. Why omit him?

BATTLER. We shall see. History, not I, must award the palm.

JUDGE. Let us omit all personalities, gentlemen. Allow me to recall you to the important point reached by Sir Midlander.

SIR O. What was that, my lord?

JUDGE. When you were challenged as to what your country would do in the event of a conflict of interest, you said frankly you did not know.

SIR O. Well, I dont.

BATTLER. And you call yourself a statesman!

SIR O. I assure you I do not. The word is hardly in use in England. I am a member of the Cabinet, and in my modest amateur way a diplomatist. When you ask me what will happen if British interests are seriously menaced you ask me to ford the stream before we come to it. We never do that in England. But when we come to the stream we ford it or bridge it or dry it up. And when we have done that it is too late to think about it. We have found that we can get on without thinking. You see, thinking is very little use unless you know the facts. And we never do know the political facts until twenty years after. Sometimes a hundred and fifty.

JUDGE. Still, Sir Midlander, you know that such an activity as thought exists.

SIR O. You alarm me, my lord. I am intensely reluctant to lose my grip of the realities of the moment and sit down to think. It is dangerous. It is unEnglish. It leads to theories, to speculative policies, to dreams and visions. If I may say so, I think my position is a more comfortable one than that of the two eminent leaders who are gracing these proceedings by their presence here today. Their remarks are most entertaining: every sentence is an epigram: I, who am only a stupid Englishman, feel quite abashed by my commonplaceness. But if you ask me what their intentions are I must frankly say that I dont know.

Where do they stand with us? I dont know. But they know what England intends. They know what to expect from us. We have no speculative plans. We shall simply stick to our beloved British Empire, and undertake any larger cares that Providence may impose on us. Meanwhile we should feel very uneasy if any other Power or combinations of Powers were to place us in a position of military or naval inferiority, especially naval inferiority. I warn you—I beg you— do not frighten us. We are a simple wellmeaning folk, easily frightened. And when we are frightened we are capable of anything, even of things we hardly care to remember afterwards. Do not drive us in that direction. Take us as we are; and let be. Pardon my dull little speech. I must not take more of your time.

GENEVA

BATTLER. Machiavelli!

BBDE. A most astute speech. But it cannot impose on us.

JUDGE. It has imposed on both of you. It is a perfectly honest speech made to you by a perfectly honest gentleman; and you both take it as an outburst of British hypocrisy.

BEGONIA. A piece of damned cheek, I call it. I wont sit here and listen to my country being insulted.

THE BETROTHED. Hear hear! Up, Camberwell!

BATTLER. What does he mean by "Up, Camberwell!"? What is Camberwell?

BEGONIA. Oh! He doesnt know what Camberwell is!

THE SECRETARY. Camberwell, Mr Battler, is a part of London which is totally indistinguishable from any other part of London, except that it is on the south side of the Thames and not on the north.

BEGONIA. What do you mean—indistinguishable? It maynt be as distangay as Mayfair; but it's better than Peckham anyhow.

BBDE. Excuse my ignorance; but what is Peckham?

BEGONIA. Oh! He doesnt know what Peckham is. These people dont know anything.

THE SECRETARY. Peckham is another part of London, adjacent to Camberwell and equally and entirely indistinguishable from it.

BEGONIA. Dont you believe him, gentlemen. He is saying that just to get a rise out of me. The people in Camberwell are the pick of south London society. The Peckham people are lower middle class: the scum of the earth.

66

BATTLER. I applaud your local patriotism, young lady; but I press for an answer to my question. What does "Up, Camberwell!" mean?

JUDGE. I think it is the south London equivalent to "Heil, Battler!"

BBDE. Ha ha ha! Ha ha! Good.

BATTLER. Am I being trifled with?

JUDGE. You may depend on me to keep order, Mr Battler. Dame Begonia is making a most valuable contribution to our proceedings. She is shewing us what we really have to deal with. Peace between the Powers of Europe on a basis of irreconcilable hostility between Camberwell and Peckham: that is our problem.

SIR O. Do not deceive yourself, my lord. Fire a shot at England; and Camberwell and Peckham will stand shoulder to shoulder against you.

BATTLER. You hear, Bardo. This Englishman is threatening us.

SIR O. Not at all. I am only telling you what will happen in certain contingencies which we sincerely wish to avoid. I am doing my best to be friendly in manner, as I certainly am in spirit. I respectfully suggest that if an impartial stranger were present his impression would be that you two gentlemen are threatening me: I might almost say bullying me.

BBDE. But we are. We shall not be thought the worse of at home for that. How are we to keep up the selfrespect of our people unless we confront the rest of the world with a battle cry? And—will you excuse a personal criticism?

SIR O. Certainly. I shall value it.

BBDE. You are very kind: you almost disarm me. But may I say that your technique is out of date? It would seem amusingly quaint in a museum, say in the rooms devoted to the eighteenth century; but of what use is it for impressing a modern crowd? And your slogans are hopelessly obsolete.

SIR O. I do not quite follow. What, exactly, do you mean by my technique?

BBDE. Your style, your gestures, the modulations of your voice. Public oratory is a fine art. Like other fine arts, it cannot be practised effectively without a laboriously acquired technique.

SIR O. But I am an experienced public speaker. My elocution has never been complained of. Like other public speakers I have taken pains to acquire a distinct articulation; and I have had the best parliamentary models before me all through my public life. I suppose—now that you put it in that way—that this constitutes a technique; but I should be sorry to think that there is anything professional about it.

BATTLER. Yes; but what a technique! I contemplated it at first with amazement, then with a curiosity which obliged me to study it—to find out what it could possibly mean. To me the object of public speaking is to propagate a burning conviction of truth and importance, and thus produce immediate action and enthusiastic faith and obedience. My technique, like that of my forerunner opposite, was invented and perfected with that object. You must admit that it has

The Judge

been wonderfully successful: your parliaments have been swept away by the mere breath of it; and we ourselves exercise a personal authority unattainable by any king, president, or minister. That is simple, natural, reasonable. But what is your technique? What is its object? Apparently its object is to destroy conviction and to paralyze action. Out of the ragbag of stale journalism and Kikkeronian Latin—

SIR O. I protest. I beg. I ask the court to protect me.

THE JUDGE. What is the matter? Protect you from what?

SIR O. From these abominable modern mispronunciations. Kikkeronian is an insult to my old school. I insist on Sisseronian.

THE BETROTHED. Hear hear!

BBDE. Take care, Ernest. This is part of the British technique. You were talking of something really important. That is dangerous. He switches you off to something of no importance whatever.

SIR O. I did not intend that, I assure you. And I cannot admit that the modern corruption of our old English pronunciation of the classics is a matter of no importance. It is a matter of supreme importance.

JUDGE. We do not question its importance, Sir Midlander; but it is outside the jurisdiction of this court; and we must not allow it to divert us from our proper business. I recall you to a specific charge of a specific crime against a specific section of the community. It is a crime of the most horrible character to drop a bomb upon a crowded city. It is a crime only a shade less diabolical to strew the sea, the common highway of all mankind, with mines that will shatter

69

and sink any ship that stumbles on them in the dark. These abominable crimes are being committed by young men—

SIR O. Under orders, my lord, and from patriotic motives.

JUDGE. No doubt. Suppose a young man picks your pocket, and, on being detected, alleges, first that somebody told him to do it, and second that he wanted your money to pay his income tax—a highly patriotic motive—would you accept that excuse?

SIR O. Ridiculous! Remember, sir, that if our young heroes are the killers, they are also the killed. They risk their own lives.

JUDGE. Let us then add a third plea to our pickpocket's defence. He runs the same risk of having his pocket picked as you. Would you accept that plea also?

SIR O. My lord: I abhor war as much as you do. But, damn it, if a fellow is coming at me to cut my throat, I must cut his if I can. Am I to allow him to kill me and ravish my wife and daughters?

JUDGE. I think that under such circumstances a plea of legitimate defence might be allowed. But what has a tussle with a murderer and a ravisher to do with laying a mine in the high seas to slaughter innocent travellers whose intentions towards yourself, your wife, and your daughters, if they have any intentions, are entirely friendly? What has it to do with dropping a bomb into the bed of a sleeping baby or a woman in childbirth?

SIR O. One feels that. It is terrible. But we cannot help its happening. We must take a practical view. It is like the London traffic. We know that so many children will be run over and killed every week. But we cannot stop the traffic because of that. Motor traffic is a part of civilized life. So is coalmining. So is railway transport. So is flying. The explosions in the mines, the collisions of the trains, the accidents in the shunting yards, the aeroplane crashes, are most dreadful; but we cannot give up flying and coalmining and railway travelling on that account. They are a part of civilized life. War is a part of civilized life. We cannot give it up because of its shocking casualties.

JUDGE. But the mine explosions and railway collisions and aeroplane crashes are not the objects of the industry. They are its accidents. They occur in spite of every possible precaution to prevent them. But war has no other object than to produce these casualties. The business and purpose of a coalminer is to hew the coal out of the earth to keep the home fires burning. But the soldier's business is to burn the homes and kill their inhabitants. That is not a part of civilization: it is a danger to it.

COMMISSAR. Come, Comrade Judge: have you never sentenced a criminal to death? Has the executioner never carried out your sentence? Is not that a very necessary part of civilization?

JUDGE. I sentence persons to death when they have committed some crime which has raised the question whether they are fit to live in human society, but not until that question has been decided against them by a careful trial at which they have every possible legal assistance and protection. This does not justify young men in slaughtering innocent persons at random. It would justify me in sentencing the young men to death if they were brought to trial. What we are here to investigate is why they are not brought to trial.

SIR O. But really, they only obey orders.

THE JUDGE. Why do you say "only"? The slaughter of human beings and the destruction of cities are not acts to be qualified by the word only. Why are the persons who give such atrocious orders not brought to trial?

SIR O. But before what court?

JUDGE. Before this court if necessary. There was a time when I might have answered "Before the judgment seat of God". But since people no longer believe that there is any such judgment seat, must we not create one before we are destroyed by the impunity and glorification of murder?

BOMBARDONE. Peace may destroy you more effectually. It is necessary for the cultivation of the human character that a field should be reserved for war. Men decay when they do not fight.

THE WIDOW. And when they fight they die.

BOMBARDONE. No no. Only a percentage, to give zest and reality to the conflict.

THE JUDGE. Would you describe a contest of a man against a machine gun, or a woman in childbirth against a cloud of mustard gas, as a fight?

BOMBARDONE. It is a peril: a deadly peril. And it is peril that educates us, not mere bayonet fencing and fisticuffs. Nations never do anything until they are in danger.

THE JEW. Is there not plenty of danger in the world without adding the danger of poison gas to it?

BBDE. Yes: there is the danger of getting your feet wet. But it has not the fighting quality that gives war its unique power over the imagination, and through the imagination over the characters and powers of mankind.

THE WIDOW. You have been a soldier. Are you the better for it? Were you not glad when your wounds took you out of the trenches and landed you in a hospital bed?

BBDE. Extremely glad. But that was part of the experience. War is not all glory and all bravery. You find out what a rotten coward you are as well as how brave you are. You learn what it is to be numbed with misery and terror as well as how to laugh at death. Ask my understudy here. He too has been a soldier. He knows.

BATTLER. We all begin as understudies, and end, perhaps, as great actors. The army was a school in which I learnt a good deal, because whoever has my capacity for learning can learn something even in the worst school. The army is the worst school, because fighting is not a whole-time-job, and in the army they pretend that it is. It ends in the discharged soldier being good for nothing until he recovers his civilian sense and the habit of thinking for himself. No, cousin: I am a man of peace; but it must be a voluntary peace, not an intimidated one. Not until I am armed to the teeth and ready to face all the world in arms is my Pacifism worth anything.

SIR O. Admirable! Precisely our British position.

73

NEWCOMER. I'm British. And what I say is that war is necessary to keep down the population.

BBDE. This man is a fool. War stimulates population. The soldier may go to his death; but he leaves behind him the pregnant woman who will replace him. Women cannot resist the soldier: they despise the coward. Death, the supreme danger, rouses life to its supreme ecstasy of love. When has a warlike race ever lacked children?

THE BETROTHED. Very romantic and all that, old man; but this notion of man on the battlefield and

woman in the home wont wash nowadays. Home was a safe place when Waterloo was fought; but today the home is the bomber's favorite mark. The soldier is safe in his trench while the woman is being blown to smithereens by her baby's cot. Kill the women; and where will your population be? Egad, you wont have any population at all.

BATTLER. This man is not a fool. If the object of war is extermination, kill the women: the men do not matter.

BBDE. The object of war is not extermination: it is the preservation of man's noblest attribute, courage. The utmost safety for women, the utmost peril for men: that is the ideal.

THE BETROTHED. I say, Signor: do you take any precautions against assassination?

BBDE. I do not encourage it; but it is one of the risks of my position. I live dangerously. It is more intense than living safely.

NEWCOMER. Your worship: these gentlemen are talking nonsense.

JUDGE. All politicians talk nonsense. You mean, I presume, that it is not the sort of nonsense you are accustomed to.

NEWCOMER. No I dont. I am accustomed to hear statesmen talking proper politics. But this about living dangerously is not proper politics: it's nonsense to me. Am I to cross the street without looking to see whether there is a bus coming? Are there to be no red and green lights? Am I to sleep in a smallpox hospital? Am I to cross the river on a tight rope instead of on a bridge? Am I to behave like a fool or a man of sense?

BBDE. You would be a much more wonderful man if you could walk on a tight rope instead of requiring several feet of solid pavement, costing years of labor to construct.

SIR O. Do you seriously propose that we should be ruled by an aristocracy of acrobats?

BBDE. Is it more impossible than your British

aristocracy of foxhunters?

SIR O. Signor: acrobats are not foxhunters.

BBDE. And gentlemen are not acrobats. But what a pity!

THE NEWCOMER. Oh, whats the use of talking to you people? Am I dreaming? Am I drunk?

BBDE. No: you are only out of your depth, my friend. And now to business. Strength. Silence. Order. I am here to meet my accusers, if any.

JUDGE. You are accused, it seems, of the murder and destruction of liberty and democracy in Europe.

BBDE. One cannot destroy what never existed. Besides, these things are not my business. My business is government. I give my people good government, as far as their folly and ignorance permit. What more do they need?

THE NEWCOMER. Why am I locked out of the parliament of Jacksonsland, to which I have been lawfully elected: tell me that.

BBDE. Presumably because you want to obstruct its work and discredit its leaders. Half a dozen such obstructionists as you could spin out to two years the work I do in ten minutes. The world can endure you no longer. Your place is in the dustbin.

THE NEWCOMER. I give up. You are too much for me when it comes to talking. But what do I care? I have my principles still. Thats my last word. Now go on and talk yourself silly.

BBDE. It is your turn now, cousin.

BATTLER. Do I stand accused? Of what, pray?

THE JEW [*springing up*] Of murder. Of an attempt to exterminate the flower of the human race.

The Betrothed

BATTLER. What do you mean?

THE JEW. I am a Jew.

BATTLER. Then what right have you in my country? I exclude you as the British exclude the Chinese in Australia, as the Americans exclude the Japanese in California.

JEW. Why do the British exclude the Chinese? Because the Chinaman is so industrious, so frugal, so trustworthy, that nobody will employ a white British workman or caretaker if there is a yellow one within reach. Why do you exclude the Jew? Because you cannot compete with his intelligence, his persistence, his foresight, his grasp of finance. It is our talents, our virtues, that you fear, not our vices.

BATTLER. And am I not excluded for my virtues? I may not set foot in England until I declare that I will do no work there and that I will return to my own country in a few weeks. In every country the foreigner is a trespasser. On every coast he is confronted by officers who say you shall not land without your passport, your visa. If you are of a certain race or color you shall not land at all. Sooner than let German soldiers march through Belgium England plunged Europe into war. Every State chooses its population and selects its blood. We say that ours shall be Nordic, not Hittite: that is all.

JEW. A Jew is a human being. Has he not a right of way and settlement everywhere upon the earth?

BATTLER. Nowhere without a passport. That is the law of nations.

JEW. I have been beaten and robbed. Is that the law of nations?

BATTLER. I am sorry, I cannot be everywhere; and all my agents are not angels.

THE JEW [*triumphantly*] Ah! Then you are NOT God Almighty, as you pretend to be. [*To the Judge*] Your honor: I am satisfied. He has admitted his guilt. [*He flings himself back into his seat*].

BATTLER. Liar. No Jew is ever satisfied. Enough. You have your warning. Keep away; and you will be neither beaten nor robbed. Keep away, I tell you. The world is wide enough for both of us. My country is not.

THE JEW. I leave myself in the hands of the court. For my race there are no frontiers. Let those who set them justify themselves.

BBDE. Mr President: if you allow Ernest to expatiate on the Jewish question we shall get no further before bed-time. He should have waited for a lead from me before meddling with it, and forcing me to banish the Jews lest my people should be swamped by the multitudes he has driven out. I say he should have waited. I must add that I have no use for leaders who do not follow me.

BATTLER. I am no follower of yours. When has a Nordic ever stooped to follow a Latin Southerner?

BBDE. You forget that my country has a north as well as a south, a north beside whose mountains your little provincial Alps are molehills. The snows, the crags, the avalanches, the bitter winds of those mountains make men, Ernest, MEN! The trippers' paradise from which you come breeds operatic tenors. You are too handsome, Ernest: you think yourself a blond beast. Ladies and gentlemen, look at him! Is he a blond beast? The blondest beast I know is the Calabrian bull. I have no desire to figure as a blond beast; but I think I could play the part more plausibly than Ernest if it were my cue to do so. I am everything that you mean by the word Nordic. He is a born Southerner; and the south is the south, whether it be the south of the Arctic circle or the south of the equator. Race is nothing: it is the number of metres above sealevel that puts steel into men. Our friend here was born at a very moderate elevation. He is an artist to his finger tips; but his favorite play as a boy was not defying avalanches. As to our races, they are so mixed that the whole human race must be descended from Abraham; for everybody who is alive now must be descended from everybody who was alive in Abraham's day. Ernest has his share in Abraham.

BATTLER. This is an intolerable insult. I demand satisfaction. I cannot punch your head because you are at least two stone heavier than I; but I will fight you with any weapon that will give me a fair chance against you.

THE JUDGE. Gentlemen: you are at the Hague, and in a Court of Justice. Duels are out of date. And your lives are too valuable to be risked in that way.

BBDE. True, your Excellency. I admit that Ernest's ancestors are totally unknown. I apologize.

BATTLER. I dont want an apology. I want satisfaction. You shall not rob me of it by apologizing. Are you a coward?

BBDE. We are both cowards, Ernest. Remember 1918. All men are cowards now.

BATTLER [*rising*] I shall go home.

WIDOW [*rising*] You shall not. Here at least we have come to the real business of this court; and you want to run away from it. If a man of you stirs I shall shoot. [*Panic*].

BOMBARDONE. Hands up, Ernest [*politely holding up his own*].

THE WIDOW. Listen to me. In my country men fight duels every day. If they refuse they become pariahs: no one will visit them or speak to them: their women folk are driven out of society as if they were criminals.

BATTLER. It was so in my country. But I stopped it.

JUDGE. Yet you want to fight a duel yourself.

BATTLER. Not for etiquette. For satisfaction.

THE WIDOW. Yes: that is what men always want. Well, look at me. I am a murderess [*general consternation*]. My husband wanted satisfaction of another kind. He got it from my dearest friend; and etiquette obliged me to kill her. In my dreams night after night she comes to me and begs me to forgive her; and I have to kill her again. I long to go mad; but I cannot: each time I do this dreadful thing I wake up with my mind clearer and clearer, and the horror of it deeper and more agonizing.

BATTLER [*flinching*] Stop this. I cannot bear it.

BBDE. Who is this woman? What right has she to be here?

WIDOW. My name is Revenge. My name is Jealousy. My name is the unwritten law that is no law. Until you have dealt with me you have done nothing.

JUDGE. You have a specific case. State it.

WIDOW. My husband has been murdered by his successor. My son must murder him if there is to be no redress but the blood feud; and I shall dream and dream and kill and kill. I call on you to condemn him.

BBDE. And condemn you.

WIDOW. I shall condemn myself. Pass your sentence on me; and I shall execute it myself, here in this court if you will.

JUDGE. But do you not understand that the judgments of this court are followed by no executions? They are moral judgments only.

WIDOW. I understand perfectly. You can point the finger of the whole world at the slayer of my husband and say "You are guilty of murder." You can put the same brand on my forehead. That is all you need do, all you can do. Then my dreams will cease and I shall kill myself. As for him, let him bear the brand as best he can.

JUDGE. That is the justice of this court. I

thank you, Señora, for your comprehension of it.

BATTLER [*distressed by the narrative*] I cannot bear this. Order that woman not to kill herself.

BBDE. No. If she has a Roman soul, who dares forbid her?

JUDGE. My authority does not go so far, Mr Battler.

BATTLER. Your authority goes as far as you dare push it and as far as it is obeyed. What authority have I? What authority has Bardo? What authority has any leader? We command and are obeyed: that is all.

BBDE. That is true, Signor judge. Authority is a sort of genius: either you have it or you have not. Either you are obeyed or torn to pieces. But in some souls and on some points there is an authority higher than any other. Of such is the Roman soul; and this is one of the points on which the Roman soul stands firm. The woman's life is in her own hands.

BATTLER. No: I tell you I cannot bear it. Forbid

her to kill herself or I will leave the court.

JUDGE. Señora: I forbid you to kill yourself. But I will sentence the slayer of your husband when his offence is proved; and by that act I will deliver you from your dreams.

WIDOW. I thank your Honor [*she sits down*].

JUDGE. Are you satisfied, Mr Battler?

BATTLER. I also thank your Honor. I am satisfied [*he resumes his seat; but his emotion has not yet quite subsided*].

BBDE. No duel then?

BATTLER. Do not torment me. [*Impatiently*] Bardo: you are a damned fool.

BBDE. [*hugely amused*] Ha ha! [*To the Judge*] The incident is closed.

An attractive and very voluble middleaged English lady enters. She is dressed as a deaconess and carries a handbag full of tracts.

DEACONESS. May I address the court? [*She goes on without waiting for a reply*]. I feel strongly that it is my duty to do so. There is a movement in the world which is also a movement in my heart. It is a movement before which all war, all unkindness, all uncharitableness, all sin and suffering will disappear and make Geneva superfluous. I speak from personal experience. I can remember many witnesses whose experience has been like my own. I——

BBDE. [*thundering at her*] Madam: you have not yet received permission to address us.

DEACONESS [*without taking the slightest notice of the interruption*] It is so simple! and the happiness it brings is so wonderful! All you have to do is to open

83

your heart to the Master.

BATTLER. What master? I am The Master.

BBDE. There are others, Ernest.

DEACONESS. If you knew what I was, and what I am, all that you are doing here would seem the idlest trifling.

BATTLER [*shouting*] Who is the Master? Name him.

DEACONESS. Not so loud, please. I am not deaf; but when one is listening to the inner voice it is not easy to catch external noises.

BATTLER. I am not an external noise. I am the leader of my people. I may become leader of many peoples. Who is this Master of whom you speak?

DEACONESS. His beloved name, sir, is Jesus. I am sure that when you were a child your mother taught you to say "All Hail, the power of Jesu's name."

THE BETROTHED. "Let angels prostrate fall."

BEGONIA. Now shut up, Billikins. I wont have you laughing at religion.

BBDE. In Ernest's country, madam, they say Heil Battler. He has abolished Jesus.

DEACONESS. How can you say that? Jesus is stronger than ever. Jesus is irresistible. You can perhaps unify your countrymen in love of yourself. But Jesus can unite the whole world in love of Him. He will live when you are dust and ashes. Can you find the way to my heart as Jesus has found it? Can you make better men and women of them as Jesus can? Can——

84

BATTLER. I have made better men and women of them. I live for nothing else. I found them defeated, humiliated, the doormats of Europe. They now hold up their heads with the proudest; and it is I, Battler, who have raised them to spit in the faces of their oppressors.

DEACONESS. Jesus does not spit in people's faces. If your people are really raised up, really saved, it is Jesus who has done it; and you, sir, are only the instrument.

NEWCOMER [*rising*] A point of order, Mister. Is this a court of justice or is it not? Are we to be interrupted by every dotty female who starts preaching at us? I protest.

DEACONESS. It is no use protesting, my friend. When He calls you must follow.

NEWCOMER. Rot. Where are the police?

THE JUDGE. The peculiarity of this court, sir, is that there are no police. The lady is raising a point of general importance: one we must settle before we can come to any fruitful conclusions here. I rule that Jesus is a party in this case.

NEWCOMER. You are as dotty as she is. I say no more. [*He resumes his seat sulkily*].

THE JEW. A party in what capacity, may I ask? I speak as a Jew, if Mr Battler will permit me.

THE JUDGE. In the capacity of a famous prophet who laid down the law in these words, "This commandment I give unto you, that ye love one another." Are you prepared to love one another?

ALL EXCEPT SIR O. [*vociferously*] No.

SIR O. Not indiscriminately.

THE BRITISH CONTINGENT. Hear hear!

SIR O. What about the Unlovables? Judas Iscariot, for instance?

DEACONESS. If he had loved the Master he would not have betrayed Him. What a proof of the truth of my message!

BBDE. Do you love Ernest here?

DEACONESS. Why of course I do, most tenderly.

BATTLER. Woman: do not presume.

BBDE. Ha! ha! ha!

DEACONESS. Why should I not love you? I am your sister in Christ. What is there to offend you in that? Is not this touchiness a great trouble to you? You can easily get rid of it. Bring it to Jesus. It will fall from you like a heavy burden; and your heart will be light, oh, so light! You have never been happy. I can see it in your face.

BBDE. He practises that terrible expression for hours every day before the looking glass; but it is not a bit natural to him. Look at my face: there you have the real thing.

DEACONESS. You have neither of you the light in your eyes of the love of the Master. There is no happiness in these expressions that you maintain so industriously. Do you not find it very tiresome to have to be making faces all day? [*Much laughter in the British section*].

BATTLER. Is this to be allowed? The woman is making fun of us.

DEACONESS. I cannot make fun. But God has ordained that when men are childish enough to fancy that they are gods they become what you call funny.

F.T.

Signor Bombardone

We cannot help laughing at them.

BBDE. Woman: if you had ever had God's work to do you would know that He never does it Himself. We are here to do it for Him. If we neglect it the world falls into the chaos called Liberty and Democracy, in which nothing is done except talk while the people perish. Well, what you call God's work, His hardest work, His political work, cannot be done by everybody: they have neither the time nor the brains nor the divine call for it. God has sent to certain persons this call. They are not chosen by the people: they must choose themselves: that is part of their inspiration. When they have dared to do this, what happens? Out of the Liberal democratic chaos comes form, purpose, order and rapid execution.

NEWCOMER. Yes, the executions come along all right. We know what dictators are.

BBDE. Yes: the triflers and twaddlers are swept away. This trifler and twaddler here can see nothing but his own danger, which raises his twaddle to a squeak of mortal terror. He does not matter. His selfchosen ruler takes him by the scruff of the neck and flings him into some island or camp where he and his like can trifle and twaddle without obstructing God's effectives. Then comes this pious lady to bid me turn to God. There is no need: God has turned to me; and to the best of my ability I shall not fail Him, in spite of all the Democratic Liberal gabblers. I have spoken. Now it is your turn, Ernest, if you have anything left to say.

BATTLER. You have said it all in your oldfashioned way, perhaps more clearly than I could have said it.

But this woman's old fairy tales do not explain me,
Ernest Battler, born a nobody, and now in command
above all kings and kaisers. For my support is no dead
Jew, but a mighty movement in the history of the
world. Impelled by it I have stretched out my hand
and lifted my country from the gutter into which you
and your allies were trampling it, and made it once
more the terror of Europe, though the danger is in
your own guilty souls and not in any malice of mine.
And mark you, the vision does not stop at my frontiers,
nor at any frontier. Do not mis-
take me: I am no soldier dreaming of military conquests: I am
what I am, and have done what I
have done, without winning a single
battle. Why is this? Because I have
snapped my fingers in the face of
all your Jewish beliefs and Roman
traditions, your futile treaties and

half hearted threats, and the vulgar abuse you have
spat at me from your platforms
and newspapers like the frightened geese you are. You must all
come my way, because I march
with the times, and march as
pioneer, not as camp follower.
As pioneer I know that the real
obstacle to human progress is
the sort of mind that has been
formed in its infancy by the Jewish Scriptures. That obstacle I
must smash through at all costs;

and so must you, Bardo, if you mean to be yourself
and not the tool of that accursed race.

COMMISSAR. I must intervene. Are we here to discuss the Jewish problem? If so, I have no business
here: my country has solved it. And we did not solve
it by badinage.

BBDE. Badinage! Are our proceedings to be described as badinage by a Bolshevist?

SECRETARY. You see how hopeless it is for us to get
any further. You have only to say the word Jew to
Herr Battler or the word Bolshevist to Signor Bombardone, and they cease to be reasonable men. You
have only to say Peckham to the representative of the
Intellectual Committee of the League of Nations to
reveal her as an irreconcilable belligerent.   You
have—

BEGONIA. Whats that
he called me? It sound-
ed awful. What does it
mean, Uncle O?

SIR O. I understood the
secretary to imply that
however largeminded
your view of the brother-
hood of mankind, you
must make an exception
in the case of Peckham.

BEGONIA. Okay. No
Peckham for me. And
mind: on that point I am
a representative woman. Sorry I interrupted. Carry
on, old man.

SECRETARY. I thank you, Dame Begonia. I must add, with great respect for the British Foreign Secretary, that you have only to say British Empire to discover that in his view the rest of the world exists only as a means of furthering the interests of that geographical expression.

SIR O. Surely the British Empire is something more than a geographical expression. But of course with me the British Empire comes first.

SECRETARY. Precisely. And as a common basis of agreement, this lady has proposed the policy of the Sermon on the Mount.

DEACONESS. Love oneanother. It is so simple.

SECRETARY. It turns out that we do not and cannot love oneanother—that the problem before us is how to establish peace among people who heartily dislike oneanother, and have very good reasons for doing so: in short, that the human race does not at present consist exclusively or even largely of likeable persons.

DEACONESS. But I assure you, that does not matter. There is a technique you have not learnt.

SIR O. What! More techniques! Madam: before your arrival, I was accused of having a technique. Can we not keep on the plain track of common-sense?

DEACONESS. But this one is so simple. You have spites. You have hatreds. You have bad tempers. All you have to do is to bring them to Jesus. He will relieve you of them. He will shew you that they are all imaginary. He will fill your hearts with love of Himself; and in that love there is eternal peace. I know so many cases. I know by my own experience.

SECRETARY. You are an amiable lady; and no doubt there are, as you say, other cases—

DEACONESS. Oh, I was not an amiable lady. I was a perfect fiend, jealous, quarrelsome, full of imaginary ailments, as touchy as Mr Battler, as bumptious as Signor Bombardone—

BATTLER. Pardon. What does touchy mean?

BBDE. I am unacquainted with the word bumptious. What am I to understand by it?

DEACONESS. Look within, look within, and you will understand. I brought it all to Jesus; and now I am happy: I am what the gentleman is kind enough to describe as amiable. Oh, why will you not do as I have done? It is so simple.

BBDE. It is made much simpler by the fact that you are protected by an efficient body of policemen with bludgeons in their pockets, madam. You have never had to govern.

DEACONESS. I have had to govern myself, sir. And I am now governed by Jesus.

JUDGE. Allow the lady the last word, Mr Leader. Proceed, Mr Secretary.

SECRETARY. No: I have said enough. You know now what an impossible job I have here as secretary to the League of Nations. To me it is agony to have to listen to all this talk, knowing as I do that nothing can come of it. Have pity on me. Let us adjourn for lunch.

JUDGE. Oh, it is not lunch time yet, Mr Secretary. We have been here less than an hour.

SECRETARY. It seems to me twenty years.

JUDGE. I am sorry, Mr Secretary. But I am waiting for the arrival of a defendant who has not yet appeared, General Flanco de Fortinbras, who is accused of having slaughtered many thousands of his fellow countrymen on grounds that have never been clearly stated.

BBDE. But he has not yet been elected Leader. He is a mere soldier.

COMMISSAR. Half Europe describes him as your valet.

BBDE. I do not keep valets. But in so far as Flanco is striving to save his country from the horrors of Communism he has my sympathy.

COMMISSAR. Which includes the help of your guns and soldiers.

BBDE. I cannot prevent honest men from joining in a crusade, as volunteers, against scoundrels and assassins.

JUDGE. You also, Mr Battler, sympathize with General Flanco?

BATTLER. I do. He has accepted my definite offer to Europe to rid it of Bolshevism if the western states will co-operate.

JUDGE. And you, Sir Midlander, can of course assure General Flanco of British support?

SIR O. [*rising*] Oh, no, no, no. I am amazed at such a misunderstanding. The British Empire has maintained the strictest neutrality. It has merely recognized General Flanco as a belligerent.

BBDE. Flanco will not come. I have not authorized him to come.

General Flanco de Fortinbras enters at the door. He is a middle aged officer, very smart, and quite conventional.

FLANCO. Pardon. Is this the International Court?

JUDGE. It is.

FLANCO. My name is Flanco de Fortinbras— General Flanco de Fortinbras. I have received a summons.

JUDGE. Quite so, General. We were expecting you. You are very welcome. Pray be seated.

The secretary places a chair between the judge and Bombardone. Flanco crosses to it.

JUDGE [*before Flanco sits down*] You know these gentlemen, I think.

FLANCO [*sitting down carelessly*] No. But I have seen many caricatures of them. No introduction is necessary.

THE JUDGE. You recognize also the British Foreign Secretary, Sir Orpheus Midlander.

Flanco immediately rises; clicks his heels; and salutes Sir Orpheus with a distinguished consideration that contrasts very significantly with his contemptuous indifference to the two leaders. Sir Orpheus, as before, waves a gracious acknowledgment of the salute. Flanco resumes his seat.

FLANCO. I have come here because it seemed the correct thing to do. I am relieved to find that His Excellency the British Foreign Secretary agrees with me.

BBDE. In what capacity are you here, may I ask?

FLANCO. Do I seem out of place between you and your fellow talker opposite? A man of action always is out of place among talkers.

BBDE. Inconceivable nothingness that you are, do you dare to class me as a talker and not a man of action?

FLANCO. Have you done anything?

BBDE. I have created an empire.

FLANCO. You mean that you have policed a place infested by savages. A child could have done it with a modern mechanized army.

BBDE. Your little military successes have gone to your head. Do not forget that they were won with my troops.

FLANCO. Your troops do fairly well under my command. We have yet to see them doing anything under yours.

BBDE. Ernest: our valet has gone stark mad.

FLANCO. Mr. Battler may be a useful civilian. I am informed that he is popular with the lower middle class. But the fate of Europe will not be decided by your scraps of Socialism.

JUDGE. May I recall you to the business of the court, gentlemen. General: you are charged with an extraordinary devastation of your own country and an indiscriminate massacre of its inhabitants.

FLANCO. That is my profession. I am a soldier; and my business is to devastate the strongholds of the enemies of my country, and slaughter their inhabitants.

NEWCOMER. Do you call the lawfully constituted democratic government of your country its enemies?

Deaconess

FLANCO. I do, sir. That government is a government of cads. I stand for a great cause; and I have not talked about it, as these two adventurers talk: I have fought for it: fought and won.

JUDGE. And what, may we ask, is the great cause?

FLANCO. I stand simply for government by gentlemen against government by cads. I stand for the religion of gentlemen against the irreligion of cads. For me there are only two classes, gentlemen and cads: only two faiths: Catholics and heretics. The horrible vulgarity called democracy has given political power to the cads and the heretics. I am determined that the world shall not be ruled by cads nor its children brought up as heretics. I maintain that all spare money should be devoted to the breeding of gentlemen. In that I have the great body of public opinion behind me. Take a plebiscite of the whole civilized world; and not a vote will be cast against me. The natural men, the farmers and peasants, will support me to a man, and to a woman. Even the peasants whom you have crowded into your towns and demoralized by street life and trade unionism, will know in their souls that I am the salvation of the world.

BBDE. A Saviour, no less! Eh?

FLANCO. Do not be profane. I am a Catholic officer and gentleman, with the beliefs, traditions, and duties of my class and my faith. I could not sit idly reading and talking whilst the civilization established by that faith and that order was being destroyed by the mob. Nobody else would do anything but read seditious pamphlets and talk, talk, talk. It was necessary to fight, fight, fight to restore order in the world. I

95

undertook that responsibility and here I am. Everybody understands my position: nobody understands the pamphlets, the three volumes of Karl Marx, the theories of the idealists, the ranting of the demagogues: in short, the caddishness of the cads. Do I make myself clear?

BBDE. Am I a cad? Is Ernest here a cad?

FLANCO. You had better not force me to be personal.

BBDE. Come! Face the question. Are we cads or gentlemen? Out with it.

FLANCO. You are certainly not gentlemen. You are freaks.

BATTLER. Freaks!

BBDE. What is a freak?

JUDGE. An organism so extraordinary as to defy classification.

BBDE. Good. I accept that.

BATTLER. So do I. I claim it.

JUDGE. Then, as time is getting on, gentlemen, had we not better come to judgment?

BATTLER. Judgment!

BBDE. Judgment!

BATTLER. What do you mean? Do you presume to judge me?

BBDE. Judge me if you dare.

FLANCO. Give judgment against me and you pass out of history as a cad.

BATTLER. You have already passed out of history as a Catholic: that is, nine tenths a Jew.

BBDE. The bee in your bonnet buzzes too much, Ernest. [*To the Judge*] What is the law?

JUDGE. Unfortunately there is no law as between

96

nations. I shall have to create it as I go along, by judicial precedents.

BATTLER. In my country I create the precedents.

BBDE. Well said, Ernest. Same here.

JUDGE. As you are not judges your precedents have no authority outside the operations of your police. You, Mr Battler, are here to answer an accusation made against you by a Jewish gentleman of unlawful arrest and imprisonment, assault, robbery, and denial of his right to live in the country of his birth. What is your defence?

BATTLER. I do not condescend to defend myself.

JEW. You mean that you have no defence. You cannot even find a Jewish lawyer to defend you, because you have driven them all from your country and left it with no better brains than your own. You have employed physical force to suppress intellect. That is the sin against the Holy Ghost. I accuse you of it.

JUDGE. What have you to say to that, Mr Battler?

BATTLER. Nothing. Men such as I am are not to be stopped by academic twaddle about intellect. But I will condescend to tell this fellow from the Ghetto that to every superior race that is faithful to itself a Messiah is sent.

DEACONESS. Oh, how true! If only you would accept him!

JUDGE. I understand you to plead divine inspiration, Mr Battler.

BATTLER. I say that my power is mystical, not rational.

BBDE. Ernest: take care. You are walking on a razor's edge between inspiration and the madness of

the beggar on horse-
back. We two are beg-
gars on horseback. For
the credit of leadership
let us ride carefully.
Leadership, we two
know, is mystical. Then
let us not pretend to un-
derstand it. God may
choose his leaders; but
he may also drop them
with a crash if they get
out of hand. Tell your-
self that every night be-
fore you get into bed,
my boy; and you may
last a while yet.

Loud applause from the British section.

BATTLER. Physician, cure yourself. You need not
prescribe for me.

JUDGE. This is very edifying, gentlemen; and I
thank you both in the name of all present. May I ask
whether this divine guidance of which you are con-
scious has any limits? Does it not imply a world State
with Mr Battler or Signor Bombardone or the British
Foreign Office at its head?

FLANCO. Certainly not in my country. A frontier
is a frontier; and there must be no monkeying with it.
Let these gentlemen manage their own countries and
leave us to manage ours.

JUDGE. Is that your view, Mr Battler?

BATTLER. No. I believe that the most advanced

race, if it breeds true, must eventually govern the world.

JUDGE. Do you agree, Sir Midlander?

SIR O. With certain reservations, yes. I do not like the term "advanced race." I greatly mistrust advanced people. In my experience they are very difficult to work with, and often most disreputable in their private lives. They seldom attend divine service. But if you will withdraw the rather unfortunate word "advanced" and substitute the race best fitted by its character—its normal, solid, everyday character—to govern justly and prosperously, then I think I agree.

JUDGE. Precisely. And now may we have your opinion, Signor Leader?

BBDE. In principle I agree. It is easy for me to do so, as my people, being a Mediterranean people, can never be subject to northern barbarians, though it can assimilate and civilize them in unlimited numbers.

JUDGE. Has the Russian gentleman anything to say?

COMMISSAR. Nothing. These gentlemen talk of their countries. But they do not own their countries. Their people do not own the land they starve in. Their countries are owned by a handful of landlords and capitalists who allow them to live in it on condition that they work like bees and keep barely enough of the honey to keep themselves miserably alive. Russia belongs to the Russians. We shall look on whilst you eat each other up. When you have done that, Russia —Holy Russia—will save the soul of the world by teaching it to feed its people instead of robbing them.

FLANCO. Did your landlords ever rob the people as

your bureaucracy now robs them to build cities and factories in the desert and to teach children to be atheists? Your country is full of conspiracies to get the old order back again. You have to shoot the conspirators by the dozen every month.

COMMISSAR. That is not many out of two hundred million people, General. Think of all the rascals you ought to shoot!

JUDGE. Pray, gentlemen, no more recriminations. Let us keep to the point of the superior race and the divine leadership. What is to happen if you disagree as to which of you is the divinely chosen leader and the superior race?

BBDE. My answer is eight million bayonets.

BATTLER. My answer is twelve million bayonets.

JUDGE. And yours, Sir Midlander?

SIR O. This sort of talk is very dangerous. Besides, men do not fight with bayonets nowadays. In fact they do not fight at all in the old sense. Mr Battler can wipe out London, Portsmouth, and all our big provincial cities in a day. We should then be obliged to wipe out Hamburg and all the eastern cities from Munster to Salzburg. Signor Bombardone can wipe out Tunis, Nice, Algiers, Marseilles, Toulouse,

Lyons, and every city south of the Loire, and oblige the French, headed by the British fleet, to wipe out Naples, Venice, Florence, Rome, and even Milan by return of post. The process can go on until the European stock of munitions and air pilots is exhausted. But it is a process by which none of us can win, and all of us must lose frightfully. Which of us dare take the responsibility of dropping the first bomb?

BATTLER. Our precautions against attack from the air are perfect.

SIR O. Ours are not, unfortunately. Nobody believes in them. I certainly do not. You must allow me to doubt the efficiency of yours.

JUDGE. And your precautions, Signor? Are they efficient?

BBDE. They do not exist. Our strength is in our willingness to die.

JUDGE. That seems to complicate murder with suicide. However, am I to take it that you are all provided with the means to effect this destruction, and to retaliate in kind if they are used against you?

SIR O. What else can we do, sir?

JUDGE. I find myself in a difficulty. I have listened to you all and watched you very attentively. You seem to me to be personally harmless human beings, capable of meeting one another and chatting on fairly pleasant terms. There is no reason why you should not be good neighbors. So far, my work of building up a body of international law by judicial precedent would seem to be simple enough. Unfortunately when any question of foreign policy arises you confront me with a black depth of scoundrelism which calls for nothing short of your immediate execution.

The Leaders and the British contingent, except the Newcomer, rise indignantly.

NEWCOMER. Hear hear! Hear hear! Hear hear! SIR O. Scoundrelism! BATTLER. Execution! BOMBARDONE. You are mad.

JUDGE. If you dislike the word execution I am willing to substitute liquidation. The word scoundrelism and its adjectives I cannot withdraw. Your objective is domination: your weapons fire and poison, starvation and ruin, extermination by every means known to science. You have reduced one another to such a condition of terror that no atrocity makes you recoil and say that you will die rather than commit it. You call this patriotism, courage, glory. There are a thousand good things to be done in your countries. They remain undone for hundreds of years; but the fire and the poison are always up to date. If this be not scoundrelism what is scoundrelism? I give you up as hopeless. Man is a failure as a political animal. The creative forces which produce him must produce something better. [*The telephone rings*]. Pardon me a moment. [*Changing countenance and holding up his hand for silence*] I am sorry to have to announce a very

gen Blanco de Fortinbras

grave piece of news.   Mr Battler's troops have invaded Ruritania.

General consternation.   All rise to their feet except Battler, who preserves an iron calm.

JUDGE. Is this true, Mr Battler?

BATTLER.   I am a man of action, not a dreamer. While you have been talking my army has been doing. Bardo: the war for the mastery of the world has begun. It is you and I, and, I presume, our friend Fortinbras, against the effete so-called democracies of which the people of Europe and America are tired.

BBDE.   Adolph: you have done this without consulting me. I warned you a year ago, when you were negotiating with a relative of Sir Orpheus here, that I could not afford another war.

FLANCO. Neither can I.

All sit down gradually, greatly relieved, except Battler.

BATTLER [*rising in great agitation*] Bardo: are you going to betray me? Remember the axis. Dare you break it?

BBDE. Damn the axis! Do you suppose I am going to ruin my country to make you emperor of the universe? You should know me better [*He resumes his seat majestically*].

BATTLER.   This is the most shameless betrayal in human history. General Flanco: you owe your victory to my aid. Will you be such a monster of ingratitude as to desert me now?

FLANCO.   I owe my victory equally to the aid of Signor Bombardone and to the masterly non-intervention policy of Sir Orpheus Midlander. I cannot prove ungrateful to either of them.

BATTLER. Well, traitors as you are, I can do without you. I can conquer Ruritania single-handed, no thanks to either of you. But where should I be if the British were not afraid to fight. Fortunately for me they do not believe in what they call brute force. [*He sits*].

SIR O. [*rising*] Pardon me. It is true that we abhor brute force, and are willing to make any sacrifice for the sake of peace—or almost any sacrifice. We understood that this was your attitude also. But I had the honor of informing you explicitly—very explicitly, Mr Battler—that Ruritania is, so to speak, our little sister, and that if you laid a finger on her we should—pardon me if in my indignant surprise at your breach of the peace I am unable to adhere to the language of diplomacy—we should be obliged to knock the stuffing out of you. That is our British method of meeting brute force.

BATTLER. What! You will fight?

SIR O. Fight, Mr Battler! We shall wipe you off the face of the earth. [*He resumes his seat*].

BATTLER. Then I am alone: *contra mundum*. Well, I have never failed yet.

FLANCO. Because you have never fought yet.

BATTLER. We shall see. I shall sweep through Ruritania like a hurricane.

COMMISSAR. Do so by all means, Comrade Battler. When you have finished you will settle with me how much of it you may keep.

BATTLER. What! You too! So the encirclement is complete.

SIR ORPHEUS. No! I cannot permit that expression.

Outflanked if you like. Hemmed in if you will have it so. I will even go so far as to say surrounded. But encircled, NO.

NEWCOMER. It puts the kybosh on Battlerism anyhow.

The telephone rings again.

ALL EXCEPT THE JUDGE. Hush. Let us hear the news. The news. The news. [*They listen with strained attention*]. Sh-sh-sh-sh-sh-.

JUDGE. What? Say that again: I must take it down: I do not understand. [*Writing as he listens*] "Astronomers report that the orbit of the earth is jumping to its next quantum. Message received at Greenwich from three American observatories. Humanity is doomed." Thank you. Goodbye. Can anyone explain this? Why is humanity doomed?

SECRETARY. It is intelligible enough, and very serious indeed.

JUDGE. It is not intelligible to me. Will you kindly explain?

SECRETARY. The orbit of the earth is the path in which it travels round the sun. As the sun is 93 million miles distant it takes us a year to get round.

JUDGE. We all know that. But the message says that the orbit is jumping to its next quantum. What does quantum mean?

SECRETARY. When orbits change they dont change gradually. They suddenly jump by distances called quantums or quanta. Nobody knows why. If the earth is jumping to a wider orbit it is taking us millions of miles further away from the sun. That will take us into the awful cold of space. The icecaps that we have on the north and south poles will spread over the whole earth. Even the polar bears will be frozen stiff. Not a trace of any sort of life known to us will be possible on this earth.

THE JEW [*rising and hurrying to the door*] Excuse me.

SECRETARY. No use running away, my friend. The icecap will overtake you wherever you go.

JUDGE. Let him alone. The shock has made him ill.

THE JEW. No: not that. I must telephone [*he goes out*].

JUDGE [*rising*] Fellow citizens: this is the end. The end of war, of law, of leaders and foreign secretaries, of judges and generals. A moment ago we were important persons: the fate of Europe seemed to depend on us. What are we now? Democracy, Fascism, Communism: how much do they matter? Your totalitarian Catholic Church: does it still seem so very totalitarian?

FLANCO. Do not blaspheme at such a moment, sir. You tell us that nothing matters. Ten minutes ago the judgment of God seemed far off: now we stand at the gates of purgatory. We have to organize absolution for millions of our people; and we have barely priests enough to do it, even if we have no converts to deal with; and we shall have many converts. We Catholics know what to do; and I have no more time to spend trifling here with men who know nothing and believe nothing. [*He moves towards the door. He stops to hear Sir O.*]

SIR O. One moment, I beg of you. This rumor must be contradicted at all costs.

COMMISSAR. How can you contradict a scientific fact?

SIR O. It must be contradicted—officially contradicted. Think of the consequences if it is believed! People will throw off all decency, all prudence. Only the Jews, with the business faculty peculiar to their race, will profit by our despair. Why has our Jewish friend just left us? To telephone, he said. Yes; but to whom is he telephoning? To his stockbroker, gentlemen. He is instructing his stockbroker to sell gilt-edged in any quantity, at any price, knowing that if this story gets about before settling day he will be able to buy it for the price of waste paper and be a millionaire until the icecap overtakes him. It must not be. I will take the necessary steps in England. The Astronomer Royal will deny this story this afternoon. You two gentlemen must see to it at once that it is officially denied in your countries.

COMMISSAR. Suppose your Astronomer Royal refuses to tell a lie. Remember: he is a man of science, not a politician.

SIR O. He is an Englishman, sir, and has some common sense. He will do his duty. Can I depend on the rest of you gentlemen?

BBDE. Can you depend on the icecap? I must go home at once. There will be a rush to the equator. My country stands right in the way of that rush. I must stop it at our frontier at any cost.

COMMISSAR. Why? Will it matter?

BBDE. I will not tolerate disorder. I will not tolerate fear. We shall die decently, stoically, steadfast at our posts, like Romans. Remember: we shall not decay: we shall stand to all eternity in cold storage. When we are discovered by some explorer from another star or another race that can live and breathe at absolute zero, he shall find my people erect at their posts like the Pompeian sentinel. You also, Ernest, must—What! Crying!! For shame, man! The world looks to us for leadership. Shall it find us in tears?

BATTLER. Let me alone. My dog Blonda will be frozen to death. My doggie! My little doggie! [*He breaks down, sobbing convulsively*].

NEWCOMER. Oh, come, old man. Dont take it so hard. I used to keep dogs myself; but I had to give it up: I couldnt bear the shortness of their lives. Youd have had to lose your little doggie some day.

Battler takes out his handkerchief and controls himself; but the Deaconess bursts into tears.

BEGONIA. Oh for God's sake, dont you start crying. You will set us all off. It's hard enough on us without that.

THE SECRETARY. Yes, maam. Take your trouble to Jesus; and set all the women a good example.

DEACONESS. But in heaven I shall lose my Jesus. There He will be a king; and there will be no more troubles and sorrows and sins to bring to Him. My life has been so happy since I found Him and came to Him a year ago! He made heaven for me on earth; and now that is all over. I cannot bear it. [*Her tears overcome her*].

NEWCOMER. Oh come come! This wont do, you know. All you people seem to think you were going to live for ever. Well, you werent. Our numbers are up; but so they were before, sooner or later. I dont complain: I havnt had such a bad time of it; and I am ready to depart, as the poet says, if it must be. In fact I must depart now and cheer up the missus. [*He rises to go*].

DEACONESS. Oh, sir, do you believe this? May it not be untrue?

NEWCOMER [*gravely*] No: it's true all right enough. If it were a priest's tale or a superstition out of the Bible I shouldnt give a snap of my fingers for it. But Science cannot be wrong. Weve got to face it. Good morning, gents.

The Newcomer goes out; and his departure breaks up the court. The Leaders and the General rise and come forward together.

DEACONESS [*to Flanco*] Oh, General, is Science always right?

FLANCO. Certainly not: it is always wrong. But I await the decision of the Church. Until that is delivered the story has no authority.

SIR O. May I suggest that you use all your influence at Rome to obtain an immediate decision from the Church against this story?

FLANCO. You shock me. The Church cannot be influenced. It knows the truth as God knows it, and will instruct us accordingly. Anyone who questions its decision will be shot. My business is to see to that. After absolution, of course. Good morning. [*He goes out*].

WIDOW. He at least has something to offer to men about to die.

COMMISSAR. Dope.

JUDGE. Why not, if they die comforted?

BATTLER. Men must learn to die undeluded.

BBDE. Flanco is dead; but he does not know it. History would have kicked him out were not History now on its deathbed.

BEGONIA. I must say I thought the general a perfect gentleman. I never wanted to kick him while he was speaking. I wanted to kick you two all the time.

THE BETROTHED. Steady, Gonny, steady! Mustnt be rude, you know.

BEGONIA. Oh, what does it matter now? As we shall all be frozen stiff presently we may as well have the satisfaction of speaking our minds until then.

THE BETROTHED. Take it easy, dear. Have a choc.

BEGONIA. No, thank you.

THE BETROTHED. I say, Uncle O: this is the first time she has ever refused a choc.

SIR O. Our valuations have changed, naturally.

THE BETROTHED. Mine havnt. You know, uncle, I think theres something in your notion of selling out and having a tremendous spree before the icecaps nip us. How does that strike you, Gonny?

BEGONIA. I dont pretend it might not have appealed to me before I represented Intellectual Co-operation. But I am a Dame of the British Empire now; and if I must die I will die like a Dame. [*She goes out*].

SIR O. Go with her, sir. And mind you behave yourself.

THE BETROTHED. Well, it does seem rather a pity. However—[*He shrugs resignedly and goes out*].

SIR O. [*to the Commissar*] Do you, sir, understand what is going to happen? My classical education did not include science.

COMMISSAR. I await instructions. The Marxian dialectic does not include the quantum theory. I must consult Moscow. [*He goes out*].

SIR O. Have these men no minds of their own? One of them must consult Rome: the other must consult Moscow. You two gentlemen fortunately have no one but yourselves to consult. Can I rely on you to do your utmost to stifle this appalling news while I return to London to consult the Cabinet?

BBDE. You can rely on nothing but this. The news has just been broadcast to all the world through the arrangements made for publicity in this court. According to you, the result will be that the people will throw off all decency and repudiate all leadership. I say that the people will want a leader as they have never wanted one before. I have taught them to order their lives: I shall teach them to order their deaths. The magnitude of the catastrophe is the measure of the leader's greatness.

SIR O. You always have a speech which sounds equal to the occasion. In England that gift would make you Prime Minister. But your very excitable countrymen may run wild.

BBDE. In that case I can do nothing but fall at the head of an attempt to stem the rush. At least one man shall stand for human courage and dignity when the race expires.

SIR O. Yes: that is a very fine attitude and quite a correct one. But have you nothing better to propose than an attitude?

BBDE. Has anyone anything better to propose than an attitude?

SIR O. I suppose not; but I feel strongly that a burst of sincerity would be a great relief.

BBDE. [*to Battler*] Give him his burst of sincerity, Ernest. Cry for your dog again. Good morning, gentlemen. [*He goes to the door*].

BATTLER [*calling after him*] You will have the honor of sharing my little dog's fate. But nobody will weep for you, Bardo.

BBDE. I hope not. I do not deal in tears. [*He strides out*].

BATTLER. What an actor!

SECRETARY. You should be a good judge of that. You have done a good deal in that line yourself.

BATTLER. We all have. But I claim to have done a little good with my acting. I will not have my work undone. We shall not stand in statuesque attitudes in Bardo's manner: we shall work to the last, and set an example to the new race of iceproof men who will follow us.

GENEVA

BERNARD SHAW

Besides, it includes your portrait, which I particularly want to have in the book.

Just to show I tried but I simply cannot ... Splendid. Put it at the end as "Title page as desired by the Author but modestly rejected by the shocked artist. It really makes an elegant design.

SIR O. Still, you know, it's no use going on making motor cars that you know will never run.

BATTLER. Yes: when the alternative is to wring our hands in despair or get drunk. We cannot work for ourselves to the last moment; but we can all work for honor. [*He goes out*].

SIR O. Wonderful luck that man has! His dog will get him into all the headlines. [*He goes out*].

JUDGE [*to the Deaconess and the widow*] Ladies: I am afraid there is nothing more to be done here.

DEACONESS [*rising*] None of you understands what this means to me, because none of you has learnt how to live. You are souls in torment, as I was until six months ago. And now I must die when I have only just learnt to live. Excuse me: I cannot bear to speak of it [*she goes out distractedly*].

JUDGE. She, at least, values her life.

SECRETARY. Yes: she belongs to some movement or other.

WIDOW [*taking her pistol from her handbag and rising*] I killed my best friend with this. I kept it to kill myself. It is useless now: God will execute His own judgment on us all. [*She throws it into the waste paper basket*]. But He is merciful; for I shall never dream again. And [*to the Secretary*] I do not belong to any movement.

He bows; and she goes out.

SECRETARY. Can you switch off?

JUDGE [*going to the table and turning a masterswitch*]

No one can hear us now. [*Returning*] Can this thing be true?

SECRETARY. No. It is utter nonsense. If the earth made a spring to a wider orbit half a minute would carry us to regions of space where we could not breathe and our blood would freeze in our veins.

JUDGE. Yet we all believed it for the moment.

SECRETARY. You have nothing to do but mention the quantum theory, and people will take your voice for the voice of Science and believe anything. It broke up this farce of a trial, at all events.

JUDGE. Not a farce, my friend. They came, these fellows. They blustered: they defied us. But they came. They came.